Earn What You're *Really* Worth

EARN
What You're
Really
WORTH

Maximize
Your Income at Any Time
in Any Market

BRIAN TRACY

Vanguard Press
A Member of the Perseus Books Group

Published by Vanguard Press
A Member of the Perseus Books Group

Designed by Brent Wilcox
Set in 11.5 point New Caledonia

Library of Congress Cataloging-in-Publication Data
Tracy, Brian.
    Earn what you're *really* worth : maximize your income in any market /
Brian Tracy.
        p.   cm.
    ISBN 978-1-59315-630-5 (hardcover : alk. paper)—
ISBN 978-1-59315-670-1 (e-book)
    1. Career development.   2. Job satisfaction.   3. Decision making.
4. Income.   I. Title.
    HF5381.T73 2012
    650.1—dc23

                                        2011042849

Vanguard Press books are available at special discounts for bulk
purchases in the U.S. by corporations, institutions, and other
organizations. For more information, please contact the Special
Markets Department at the Perseus Books Group, 2300 Chestnut
Street, Suite 200, Philadelphia, PA 19103, or call (800) 810-4145,
ext. 5000, or e-mail special.markets@perseusbooks.com.

10 9 8 7 6 5 4 3 2 1

This book is dedicated to Tayah Waterhouse, Chelsea Frederick, and Julie Dominy, my friends and partners, whose ability to tap into their potentials and truly earn what they are really worth is a wonderful inspiration to all of us.

CONTENTS

You Have Chosen Your Current Income

> Formulate and stamp indelibly on your mind a mental picture of yourself as succeeding. Hold this picture tenaciously. Never permit it to fade. Your mind will seek to develop the picture. . . . Do not build up obstacles in your imagination.
>
> **—NORMAN VINCENT PEALE**

You are earning today exactly the amount that you have decided to earn, no more and no less. You are where you are financially because you have chosen to be there. Only you. No one else.

What this means, in terms of income, is that whatever you are earning today is the amount that you have *decided* to earn. Not a penny more, not a penny less.

You have decided to earn this amount as a result of your actions and as a result of your *inactions*. There are specific actions you have taken to get your income to the point where it is today.

And there are actions that you have failed to take that have caused your income to stay far below what you are truly capable of earning. Whatever you are earning today, you have decided to earn that amount.

When I first heard this idea, that I was determining my own income, I was shocked and angry. I denied it vigorously. "That's not true," I said. "No one would choose to earn *this* amount, and worry about money all the time!"

I blamed my low income on my parents, my education, my boss, my company, my industry, the competition, and the economy. Then I looked around me, and realized that there were hundreds and even thousands of people who had the same problems and limitations I did but who were earning far more than I was and living much better lives.

I finally accepted that I was where I was and what I was because of *me*. If I was not happy about my life and my income, there was only one person in the world who could change it—me. As the song says, it was "me, O Lord, standing in the need of prayer." This awakening changed my life.

Five years later, I had increased my income ten times! I went from a rented apartment with rented furniture to my own home with my own dream car, a Mercedes-Benz SL350, parked in my spacious double garage. My whole life was different, and yours can be as well.

Your Earning Ability

Your most valuable financial asset is your *earning ability*, your ability to earn money. This can be defined as your ability to get results that people will pay you for. Unless you are already rich, your earning ability, or *earning power*, represents 80 to 90 percent of your financial value.

Properly applied to the marketplace, your earning ability is like a water well. By maximizing your earning ability through getting results that people will pay you for, you can pump tens of thousands of dollars a year into your pocket. All your knowledge, education, skills, and experience in life have contributed to the person you are today and to this ability to get results for which someone will pay good money.

Your earning ability is like farmland—if you don't take excellent care of it, if you don't fertilize it, and cultivate it, and water it on a regular basis, it soon loses its ability to produce the kind of harvest that you desire. Successful men and women are those who are extremely aware of the importance and value of their earning ability. They work every day to keep it increasing in productive value, and current with the demands of the marketplace.

An Appreciating Asset

Your earning ability, like any asset, can be either *appreciating* or *depreciating*. It can be regularly increasing in value, enabling you to earn more and more with each passing year. Or it can be a *depreciating* asset, losing value as the markets change and your skills become less and less in demand.

Here is the hard truth: if you are not becoming more and more valuable, by continuously and aggressively upgrading your skills, you are *automatically* falling behind. If your earning ability is not appreciating, it is automatically depreciating. There are

millions of unemployed people today who have let their earning
ability decline so far that no one will hire them to get the few results they are still capable of generating.

Make a Decision

What is the key to increasing your income? Make a decision! Make
a decision, from this day forward, that you are going to earn the
amount of money that you are truly capable of earning. Make a decision that you are going to take complete control of your career
and your income so you can survive and thrive in any economy.

Make a decision today that you are going to *double your income* and then double it again. Make a decision that you are going
to earn more and more until you fulfill your true potential as an
earning machine.

In the pages ahead, I will give you a series of practical, proven
strategies, methods, and techniques that you can use immediately
to begin to earn what you are really worth. The best news is that
the amount that you are truly worth is vastly *higher* than anything
you have ever enjoyed up to the current day.

Remember, it doesn't matter where you're coming from; all
that really matters is where you're *going*. And where you're going
is only limited by your imagination.

Your very highest income lies in the future. Your very best accomplishments lie in the future. Your proudest achievements lie
in the future. Your happiest moments lie in the future. The greatest successes of your life are still to come. This book will show
you how to get them.

CHAPTER ONE

The New Normal

Genius is 1 percent inspiration and 99 percent perspiration. Accordingly, a "genius" is often merely a talented person who has done all of his or her homework.

—THOMAS EDISON

Welcome to the "new normal" of work, employment, and career success.

We have moved in just a few years from an age of *affluence*, when the stock market was booming, the unemployment rate was below 5 percent, and people were becoming millionaires and billionaires all around us, to a new age of *turbulence*, when all bets are off. Today, the economic situation has changed completely, and it is not going to change back in our lifetimes.

We are going through a massive paradigm shift. When a shift like this in thinking or in society takes place, only a few people recognize that it is occurring. Most people are stuck in a comfort zone where they keep on doing the same old things in the same old way, simply assuming that the economic and financial meltdown of 2007–2010 was a bump in the road, and that everything will soon get back to normal.

They are right, but the definition of *normal* has changed. From this day forward, if you want to succeed and achieve everything that is possible for you, you are going to have to work smarter and more diligently than ever before. To move to the top of your field, you are going to have to start a little earlier, work a little harder, and stay a little later.

The Race Is On

The fact is that there is a race on, and you are in it. If you don't pick up the pace, other people will. Your competitors will increase the speed at which they are moving and leave you far behind.

There is an old saying, "Shirtsleeves to shirtsleeves in three generations." What this refers to is the common story of a poor entrepreneur starting a business and eventually becoming financially successful, before handing it off to his children. They mismanage the business and squander the money because they don't know how the money was made in the first place. This makes it necessary for their children to start over again as workers and employees. "Shirtsleeves to shirtsleeves in three generations" is the common story of how wealth is earned and lost over and over again.

After World War II, the United States was the "last man standing." Most people living today have no memory of the Great Depression that took place between 1929 and 1941, reaching an unemployment rate of 28 percent and persisting year after year in spite of every conceivable góvernment program attempting to bring back prosperity.

After a decade of disastrous government policies, the enormous industrial and labor demands of World War II pulled the United States out of the Depression. Most business people and economists thought the United States would plunge right back into depression as soon as the war was over. Fortunately, that didn't happen.

The Growth of Affluence

Nonetheless, the shirtsleeves generations of the 1930s and 1940s went to work in the 1950s and 1960s to take advantage of America's rare place in the world economy. They started and built businesses, created jobs, produced affluence and opportunity, exploded the number of products and services available, and made the United States the economic powerhouse of the world, generating 40 percent of the gross world product. This was an incredible achievement in human history—one that has never been seen before or since.

But by 1970, when the baby-boomer generation began to enter the workforce, the rest of the world had caught up, especially Germany and Japan. This second generation, never having experienced anything but a rising tide of abundance, began to see high living standards and a growing economy, with countless opportunities for success and affluence, as the natural and normal state of affairs. Everyone hoped, or expected, to be a millionaire by the time he or she was thirty.

Alas! Just as in every civilization throughout the centuries, this affluent generation, the ones we call baby boomers, began to develop a sense of entitlement. They began to believe that if you were born in America, you were entitled to a "fat life."

The Most Popular Destination

The word about American affluence and opportunity went out across the globe like a jungle telegraph, and eventually people from all over the world began to flow toward the United States, both legally and illegally, to get a piece of the action. America became the most popular destination in the world, and it still is to most people. It is said that the most valuable piece of paper on earth is an American green card entitling a foreigner to live and work in the United States legally.

Unfortunately, we have become soft as a people. The vast majority of Americans expect to get something for nothing, money that they have not earned and do not deserve. They look for fast, easy ways to get rich and are suckers for the next "get rich quick" scheme that comes down the pike. The very idea of making money the old-fashioned way, by earning it, is viewed as unfair and unkind.

Economist Joseph Schumpeter spoke about "gales of creative destruction," predicting never-ending economic turbulence and change that would alter our economy. Today, there are three factors that are totally disrupting our economic lives and futures, and causing disruptions that are unceasing, inevitable, and unpredictable.

Information Explosion

The first of these is *information*. The amount of information in the world is now doubling every two or three years. By 2020, some people say that the total written information in the world will be doubling every seventy-two days! Nearly a million books and millions of articles are published in the English language alone each year. And just one new piece of information that affects your job, career, or profession can have a significant impact on your future, either for better or for worse.

Technological Revolution

The second factor driving change today is the explosion of *technology*. It is said that new technology has a shelf life of six months. If it exists, it's probably already obsolete.

Throughout the world—in the United States, and especially in Asia and Europe—some of the smartest, most ambitious, and most determined inventors, entrepreneurs, innovators, and creators are working night and day to develop new disruptive technologies that lead to the creation of new industries and the destruction of old ones.

Increased Competition

The third factor affecting your life and driving change is *competition*. As corporate consultant Marshall Goldsmith says, "The three factors that will most determine your future are competition, competition, and competition."

Each of these three factors impacts the others. When you multiply information by technology by competition, you get a rate of change that is accelerating, sweeping everything before it, and making products, services, ideas, and technologies obsolete often before they get off the drawing board. And if anything, this rate of change is going to increase in the years ahead.

Alice in Wonderland

Many people are living an "Alice in Wonderland" existence, feeling themselves in a parallel world, looking around and not really understanding what is going on. In the book *Through the Looking-Glass*, by Lewis Carroll, there is a scene in which Alice says to the Red Queen after they've been running in place together for a while, "In *our* country, you'd generally get to somewhere else—if you ran very fast for a long time, as we've been doing."

To which the Red Queen, still running in place, replies, "*Here*, you see, it takes all the running *you* can do, to keep in the same place. If you want to get somewhere else, you must run at least twice as fast as that!" In our lives, the new normal is that we will have to run twice as fast just to stay in the same place, personally, nationally, and internationally. We are going to have to work a lot harder and a lot smarter than has ever been required of us before. The rest of the world has caught up with us and wants to enjoy the same standard of living that we do. The only difference is that they are willing to work for it, twelve to sixteen hours a day, six days a week, and more. They are totally determined to "eat our lunch."

Fat and Lazy

Most people outside the United States, especially in Asia, think that Americans have grown fat and lazy, and that the days of American dominance are over. This belief is too true in the case of too many Americans. Probably 80 percent of the population is coasting. They are content to do an average job and live an average life. But the problem with coasting is that you can only do it in one direction: downhill!

The good news is that there are doors opening around you. Because of the incredible turbulence and rapid rate of change in today's world, there are countless possibilities for you to start and build a great life, achieve all your goals, and become financially independent, if not rich, in the years ahead.

But with the new game, the rules have changed. In this book you are going to learn the *new* rules for success, promotion, affluence, and achievement. You will learn some of the most powerful ideas and insights practiced by the most successful men and women in every field. You will learn how to take complete control of your working life and your future, earn more money than you ever thought possible, and accomplish more than almost anyone around you.

The Power of Initiative

One of the fastest ways to put your career onto the fast track, to become more valuable, and to attract the support of people who can help you to earn more money, is to develop and maintain the *power of initiative*. Always look for new, better, faster, cheaper ways to create value, to get the job done, and to go beyond what anyone expects. Seize the bull by the horns, go the extra mile, volunteer for greater responsibility, and always do more than you're paid for.

The world belongs to those who reach out and grab it with both hands. It belongs to those who do something rather than just wish and hope, and plan and pray, and intend to do something someday, when everything is just right.

Successful people are not necessarily those who make the right decisions all the time. No one can do that, no matter how smart he or she is. But once successful people have made a decision, they take action. They begin moving toward their objectives step by step. As they do, they begin to get feedback or signals that enable them to self-correct. They continually get new information that enables them to adjust their plans in large and small ways.

Make Continual Course Corrections

Life is a process of trial and error and course corrections. For example, when an airplane leaves Chicago for Los Angeles, it is off course 99 percent of the time. This is normal, and natural, and to be expected. The pilot makes continual course corrections, a little to the north, a little to the south, to higher and to lower altitudes. The pilot continually adjusts direction and throttle. And sure enough, several hours later the plane touches down at exactly the time predicted when it first became airborne upon leaving Chicago. The entire journey has been a process of approximations and course adjustments. This is the story of your life as well.

The point is that there are no guarantees in life. Everything you do—even crossing the street—is filled with uncertainty. You can never be completely sure that any action or behavior of yours is going to bring about the desired result. There is always a risk. And where there is risk, there is fear. And whatever you think about grows in your mind and heart. People who think constantly about the risks involved in any undertaking soon become preoccupied with fears, and doubts, and anxieties that conspire to hold them back from trying in the first place.

Launch Toward Your Goals

At Babson College, in a twelve-year study into the subsequent careers of the graduates of the school's MBA program in entrepreneurship, researchers concluded that those graduates who were successful achieved their goals because of their use of the "Corridor Principle."

The Babson researchers likened the achievement of business success to proceeding down a corridor. Each of us stands at the entrance to this corridor, looking into the darkness, and we see the corridor disappear into the distance. The researchers said that the difference between the successes and the failures in their study could be summarized by one word: *launch*!

Successful people were willing to launch themselves down the corridor of opportunity without any guarantee of what would occur. They were willing to risk uncertainty and overcome the normal fears and doubts that hold the great majority in place.

New Doors of Opportunity

What the Babson researchers discovered was that as you move down the corridor of life, new doors of opportunity open up on both sides of you. However, you will not see those doors if you are not already in motion, moving forward down the corridor. The opportunities will not open up for you if you wait for some assurance before stepping out in faith and taking action.

The Confucian saying "A journey of a thousand leagues begins with a single step" simply means that great accomplishments begin with your willingness to face the inevitable uncertainty of any new enterprise and step out boldly in the direction of your goal. It begins with your taking initiative in the first place.

The Vacuum Principle

Not long ago, a couple came to me with a problem. The husband was working for a company owned by his family and he was bitterly unhappy. The company was full of politics, and backbiting, and negativity, and he was stressed out and hated his job. He wanted to do something else but had no job offers or potential alternatives to his current position. He asked me for my advice on what to do.

I explained to him that there is a Vacuum Principle of Prosperity, which says that when you create a vacuum of any kind, nature rushes in to fill it. In his case, this meant that as long as he stayed at his current job, there was no way that other opportunities could find him or that he could recognize other possibilities. I told him to take a giant leap of faith and just walk away from his current job with no lifeline or safety net. I assured him that if he did, all kinds of possibilities would open up for him that he simply couldn't see while he was locked up in his current situation.

He took my advice; he quit his job. The members of his family became very angry and told him that he would be unemployable outside of their business. But he stuck to his guns. He went home, took a few days off, and began to think about his experience and his skills and how they could best be applied to other jobs in other companies.

Within two weeks, without raising a finger, he had two job offers from other companies, both paying substantially more than he was earning working for his family firm and both offering all kinds of opportunities that were vastly superior to those at the job he had walked away from. As soon as the word had gotten out in the marketplace that he was available, other company owners, having worked with him and his company in the past, were eager to open doors for him. As he moved down the corridor of life, he began to see possibilities that he had been missing completely by limiting himself to where he was.

Try More Things

If you want to be more successful faster, just *do or try more things.* Take more actions. Get busier. Start a little earlier; work a little harder; stay a little later. Put the odds in your favor. According to the law of probability, the more things you try, the more likely it is that you will try the one thing that will make all the difference.

Luck is quite predictable. If you want more luck, take more chances. Show up more often. The harder you work, the luckier you get.

Tom Peters, the bestselling author of *In Search of Excellence* and other business books, found that a key quality of the top executives in his study was a "bias for action." Their motto seemed to be "Ready, aim, fire." Their attitude toward business was summarized in the words "Do it, fix it, try it." They had realized that the future belongs to the action-oriented, to the risk takers.

Top people know that, as Gen. Douglas MacArthur once said, "There is no security on this earth; there is only opportunity." And the interesting discovery is this: if you seek for opportunity, you'll end up with all the security you need. However, if you seek for security, you'll end up with neither opportunity nor security. The proof of this is all around us, in the downsizing and reconstructing of corporations, where thousands of men and women who sought security are finding themselves unemployed for long periods of time.

The Momentum Principle

There is a Momentum Principle of Success, which is very important to you. It's derived from two physical laws, the law of inertia and the law of momentum, and it applies equally well to everything that you accomplish and that you fail to accomplish.

In physics the first law of motion states: "A body in motion tends to remain in motion unless acted upon by an outside force; a body at rest tends to remain at rest unless acted upon by an outside force."

The law of momentum says that it may take a lot of energy to start moving initially, but then it takes much less energy to keep moving. It requires tremendous discipline to start a new business or activity, but once you get going, it is easier to keep going. As Einstein said, "Nothing happens until something moves." Nothing happens until you move, as well.

Get Going and Keep Going

In the simplest terms, as they apply to you and your life these laws say that once you get started, once you get into motion toward something that is important to you, it's much easier to continue making progress than to have to start again if you stop somewhere along the way.

When you look at successful people, you find that they are very much like the plate spinners in vaudeville acts. They get things started; they get the plates spinning. They then keep them spinning, knowing that if a plate falls off or something comes to a halt, it's much harder to get it restarted than it is to keep it going in the first place.

Once you have a goal and a plan, get going! And once you start moving toward your goal, don't stop. Do something every day to move you closer to your goal. Don't let the size of the goal or the amount of time required to accomplish it faze you or hold you back.

During your planning process, break down the goal into small tasks and activities that you can engage in every day. You don't have to do a lot, but every day, every week, every month you should be making progress, by completing your predetermined tasks and activities, in the direction of your clearly defined objectives.

Discipline Yourself Daily

Here is where the rubber meets the road. The most important single quality for success is *self-discipline*. As Elbert Hubbard defines it, self-discipline is the ability to make yourself do what you should do, when you should do it, whether you feel like it or not.

Let me break down that definition of self-discipline. First, there's making yourself do what you should do. This means that you have to use strength and willpower to force yourself into motion, to break the power of inertia that holds you back. Second, there's doing what you should do when you should do it. This means that you make a plan, set a schedule, and then do what you say you'll do. You do it when you say you'll do it. You keep your promises to yourself and to others.

The third part of this definition is *whether you feel like it or not.* You see, anyone can do anything if he or she feels like it, if he or she wants to do it because it feels good, if he or she is well rested and has lots of time. However, the true test of character is when you do something that you know you must do whether you feel like it or not—especially when you don't like it at all.

In fact, you can tell how badly you really want something and what you're really made of as a person by how capable you are of taking action in the direction of your goals and dreams even when you feel tired, and discouraged, and disappointed, and you don't seem to be making any progress. Very often, this is the exact time when you will break through to great achievement.

Ralph Waldo Emerson once wrote, "When it is darkest, men see the stars." Your ability to endure, to continue taking action, step by step, in the direction of your dreams, is what will ultimately ensure your success. If you keep on keeping on, nothing can stop you.

If you have the discipline to take continual action, to practice the power of initiative, your eventual success is guaranteed.

Action Exercises:

1. Identify the most important area of your work where new information is forcing you to make changes.
2. Determine the most significant technological breakthrough that is having, and will have, an effect on your income.
3. Identify the competition that is having the greatest effect on your industry and your income.
4. Decide upon one key discipline that you need to develop to move ahead faster in your career.
5. Choose one action that you could take immediately to improve your career or income.
6. Identify the biggest single opportunity for you in your job or industry today.
7. Select one area where you are going to take initiative to improve your work and increase your income.

Your Personal Service Corporation

> The most delightful surprise in life is to suddenly
> recognize your own worth.
>
> —MAXWELL MALTZ

An attitude of self-responsibility goes hand in hand with success, happiness, self-control, and high earnings in every area of life. In a detailed study the researchers discovered that the top 3 percent of workers in every field saw themselves as *self-employed*. They acted as if they personally owned the companies they worked for. They accepted responsibility for everything that happened to their companies as well as for results. When you develop this attitude, you immediately move onto the fast track in your career.

The biggest mistake you can make is to ever think that you work for anyone other than yourself. No matter who signs your paycheck, you are always self-employed, from the time you take your first job until the day you retire. You are the head of an entrepreneurial enterprise with one employee—yourself—responsible for selling one product—your personal services.

Put another way, you are the president of your own personal service corporation, *You, Inc.* You are the chief executive officer of your own life. You are completely responsible for this business of your life and for everything that happens to both it and you. You are in charge of production, marketing, quality, finance, and research and development.

You Write Your Own Paycheck

You ultimately determine your own salary and write your own paycheck. If you are not happy with the amount that you are earning, you can go to the nearest mirror and negotiate with your boss. We are each where we are and what we are in the world of work because that is where and what we have decided to be. If we are not happy with any part of our careers, it is up to us to make whatever changes are necessary to bring about a better state of affairs.

When you are the president of your own personal service corporation, everything that affects the business you work for affects your personal business as well. You no longer have the luxury of standing aside and looking at the rate of change, thinking that it affects other people but not you. Losers say, "That's not my job." Winners say, "This is my company; everything is *my* job."

Every innovation, discovery, and paradigm shift in modern business is as applicable to you as it is to a multi-billion-dollar corporation. Every piece of information being generated by management and business thinkers that can affect your business in some way relates to you.

The men and women who will survive and thrive in the years ahead are those who are continually looking for ideas and insights that they can use to be faster, more flexible, and more effective in their work on a day-to-day basis.

As is the case for the presidents of all high-achieving companies, your goal is to be a *market leader*. In fact, if you are not committed to being the best in your field, you are unconsciously accepting mediocrity. If you are not getting better, you are probably getting *worse*. If you are not committed to being one of the top 10 percent of the people in your field, you will end up somewhere far below.

Start With Your Values

One of the most important findings in the last few years is that defining *core values* is a vital step for both successful individuals and profitable businesses. Companies that have clear, written values, and mission statements based on those values, are consistently more profitable than those that do not. Likewise, individuals who have clear core values and personal mission statements seem to be far more effective and successful than those who do not.

You can dramatically improve the quality of your life by thinking through and deciding what your values really are, or should be, and then committing yourself to live consistently by those values, no matter what the external circumstances may be.

Values Clarification

Shortly after we got married, my wife and I sat down one weekend and wrote out all the values that we believed in and were committed to. We came up with a list of 163 values. We very quickly realized that this list was far too large for us to use as the basis for decision-making. So we cut the list down to about five key values. We then dedicated ourselves to defining what they meant to us and to organizing our lives around them. This has made an enormous difference in everything that we have accomplished in the last few years. You should do the same.

Once you have determined your own personal values, you can work toward organizing your life around them. Values give you a foundation upon which you can make your decisions. Whenever you are confronted with a choice, you can evaluate the alternatives based on what you most value.

What are *your* core values? What do you believe in? What do you stand for? What will you *not* stand for?

Market Research

Here's a good exercise for you: Imagine that a market research firm is going to come into your community and do a study on you. The researchers are going to ask all the people who know you, your family, friends, customers, coworkers, and bosses, to give their opinions of you. They are going to ask all your contacts what kind of person you are. They are going to ask what sort of values you have and what you stand for as an individual. They are going to ask about your philosophy and beliefs, based on your words and actions. They are going to work up a complete profile on you to be broadcast on national television.

Based on this scenario, consider these questions: What would the people around you say about you to the researchers?

How would they describe you? What would they say are your values based on the way you act and the way you treat other people? What would they say about the quality of work you do? Most importantly, how would you like them to talk about you in the future?

Your Reputation Is Everything

Successful companies almost invariably take the time to sit down and think through the answers to these questions. Dr. Theodore Levitt of the Harvard Business School said that a company's reputation is its most valuable asset in a competitive marketplace. Levitt defined *reputation* as "how the company is described by others."

Any company that can positively influence the way customers think and talk about it to others has accomplished a tremendous feat. It is easier for a company to charge more and sell more in a competitive market when it has an excellent reputation. A company's reputation builds slowly and changes slowly. Its products, processes, and people may all change over time, but its reputation can last for decades.

It is the same with you. What kind of reputation do you have in your marketplace, among the people you know and work with? And what kind of reputation would you like to have in the future?

Develop a Personal Mission Statement

Once you have determined your core values, you can develop your mission statement. A mission statement is a future-tense description, based on your values, of the kind of person or corporation that you would ideally like to be in three to five years.

Your core values and the mission statement that flows from them then become your operating principles for everything you do. You commit all your resources to living consistently with them.

A mission has both a *measure* and a *method*. It is aimed at achieving something for others, especially in business.

Your Own Mission Statement

You can write your own mission statement by completing the following sentence:

"My mission is to (do what you intend to do to improve the life or work of someone), which I achieve by (what you intend to do to achieve that improvement), and I measure success by when I (achieve the measure you will use to determine whether you have completed your mission)."

Example: My mission is to make a valuable contribution to the success of my company, which I achieve by rendering the highest quality and quantity of work possible at all times, and I measure success by when I am paid more and promoted faster than others because of the value of my contribution."

The Seven Rs of Personal Management

With your values and your mission statement clear, you can further your personal effort to become highly paid by engaging in the seven Rs of modern management. These seven Rs are *rethinking, reevaluating, reorganizing, restructuring, reengineering, reinventing,* and *refocusing.*

In *rethinking,* you take time on a regular basis to think about who you are and where you are going, especially when you are discontented for any reason. Since everything is changing so rapidly around you, more options are available to you now than ever before. And because it is very likely that you are going to be doing something completely different in a few years anyway, you can begin thinking today about where you want to be in the future. You can rethink and re-plan your entire career.

Reevaluate Your Situation

Reevaluating is the process of standing back and looking at yourself in terms of the marketplace. Whenever you experience stress, frustration, or continual roadblocks in your work or career, you need to take time to reevaluate your situation and be sure that you are on the right track.

Your problems may be caused by your not working at the right job for you, or working at the wrong company, or working with the wrong people. Your dissatisfaction may be caused by your selling a product or service that is wrong for you, or for many other reasons. Perhaps your heart is no longer in your work. It gives you little or no pleasure. Sometimes, the very best thing to do in a situation like this is to change the work you are doing or the company for which you are working, so that your work life is more consistent with your talents, abilities, desires, and values.

Reorganize Your Life

In *reorganization*, you examine your daily activities and question whether or not you should be doing things differently if you want to get better results. Look for ways to work with greater efficiency and perform your tasks more effectively. Continually try to increase your output relative to your input of time and money.

Restructure Your Activities

In *restructuring*, you continually look at the specific things you do that contribute the most value to your company and to your customers. You focus more and more of your time and talent on the 20 percent of your activities that contribute 80 percent of the value of all the things that you do. You concentrate on those activities that represent the highest payoff for everyone involved.

Reengineer Your Career

In *reengineering* your personal service corporation, you stand back and look at the entire process of your work, from the first thing you do in the morning to the actual results that you get for your company or your customer. You analyze this process and look for ways to streamline it by reducing steps, consolidating activities, outsourcing parts of the work, and even changing the process completely so that you can achieve the same or better results with less time and fewer resources. Reengineering is an ongoing process of simplifying your work and your activities so that you can get more done in less time.

Reinvent Yourself Regularly

In *reinventing*, you stand back from your work and imagine starting over again. Imagine that your job or industry disappeared completely. Imagine for a moment that you had to move across the street or across the country and begin your career or your business all over. What would you do differently? Where do you want to be in your career in three to five years? What changes would you have to make in reinventing your business to create the future that you desire?

One of the best ways to reinvent yourself is to determine what it is that you really enjoy doing more than anything else, and then to begin figuring out how you can find or create a job doing more of it.

Refocus Your Energies

The final R stands for *refocusing*. This is really the key to the future. It is your ability to concentrate your energies single-mindedly on doing those few things that make all the difference in your life.

In most cases, people are unsuccessful because they spend too much time doing things that contribute little to their lives. They spend more and more time doing things that have less and less value. On the other hand, highly successful people do not do a lot of things, but the few things they do, they do extremely well.

This seems to be the secret to great success and achievement in every area of life.

Become a Master of Change

The advantage of practicing the seven Rs, of focusing on the disciplines that enable you to be a leader in your field and master the forces of change, is that they allow you to *regain control* over your present and future. With a sense of control comes a feeling of personal power and greater self-confidence. When you determine your own life and future, rather than allowing them to be determined by the unpredictable winds of change, you feel happier, healthier, and more powerful in everything you do.

Continually think of yourself as the president of your own personal service corporation. See yourself as being in charge of your own life. You are responsible. When you begin to see yourself as an active participant in the dynamic world around you, you take full control of your own destiny. You become the architect of your own future and the primary creative force in your own life.

Action Exercises:
1. Determine which are the three to five values that are most important to you, the ideals and virtues you stand for and will not compromise.
2. Write out your business mission statement using the template contained in this chapter.
3. Decide on the words that you would like others to use to describe you, and then organize your life so that you live by and practice those words.

4. Reevaluate your life and make sure that what you are doing is consistent with the best life you could be living, or else be prepared to make changes.
5. Reengineer your life by continually seeking ways to simplify your work by eliminating time-wasting or unnecessary activities.
6. Restructure your work regularly to be sure that you are always working on those tasks that represent the greatest value to yourself and your business.
7. Refocus your time, talents, and energies on those activities that produce the most results in your work.

CHAPTER THREE

Increase Your Earning Potential

There are risks and costs to a plan of action. But
they are far less than the long-range risks and costs
of comfortable inaction.

—JOHN F. KENNEDY

Throughout most of human history, we have been accustomed to evolution, or the gradual progression of events in a straight line. Sometimes the process of change has been faster and sometimes it has been slower, but it has almost always seemed to be progressive, moving forward, from one step to the next, allowing you sufficient time for planning, predicting, and changing.

Today, however, the rate of change is not only faster than ever before, but it is *discontinuous*. It is taking place in a variety of unconnected areas and affecting each of us in a multitude of unexpected ways. Changes in information technology are happening separately from changes in medicine, changes in transportation, changes in education, changes in politics, and changes in global competition.

Changes in family formation and relationships are happening separately from the rise and fall of new businesses and industries in different parts of the country and the world. And if anything, this rate of accelerated, discontinuous change is increasing. As a result, most of us are already suffering from what Alvin Toffler once called "future shock."

Your choice of a career, and a job within that career, is one of the most important decisions you ever make. Unfortunately, most people drift into their jobs, accepting whatever is offered to them at the time and then allowing other people to determine what they will do, where they will do it, how they will do it, and how much they will be paid for it. The company and the boss become very much like an extension of the mother and the father, taking care of everything. This creates a natural inertia, a resistance to any change in direction or speed that carries most people onward through their careers, month after month and year after year.

Don't Settle for Less

But this is not for you. Your goal is to get a great job that you really enjoy and that pays you the very most that you can possibly earn in exchange for your mental, emotional, and physical energies. The good news is that, no matter your situation, you are not trapped. You have free will. You have choices. There are countless jobs that you can perform with your brains and abilities.

We have moved from an era of lifelong employment to an era of lifelong *employability*. No matter who signs your paycheck, you are your own boss, completely responsible for every part of your work and personal life. In the long run you determine how much you get paid and everything that happens to you. You are responsible.

One of the key questions the most valuable people in any company ask is, How can I increase the value of my service to my company today?

You should ask and answer that question over and over, and whatever your answer, you should put it into action immediately. Your first job in your work is to become valuable. Your second job is to become *indispensable*. This question will help you to achieve both goals.

The Market Is Tough and Getting Tougher

The marketplace is a stern taskmaster. Today, excellence, quality, and value are absolutely essential elements of any product or service, and of the work of any person. Your earning ability is largely determined by the perception of excellence, quality, and value that others have of you and what you do.

The market only pays excellent rewards for excellent performance. It pays average rewards for average performance, and it pays below-average rewards (or unemployment) for below-average performance. Customers today want the very most, and the very best, on the very best terms for the very least amount of money. Only those individuals and companies that provide absolutely excellent products and services at absolutely excellent prices will survive. It's not personal; it's just the way our economy works.

To earn more, you must learn more. You are maxed out today at your current level of knowledge and skill. However much you are earning at this moment is the maximum you can earn without learning and practicing something new and different.

Take Charge of Your Career

You have been designed by nature to do certain things and perform certain tasks extraordinarily well. You have been engineered for success from the very beginning. You have within you deep reservoirs of talent and ability that you have never tapped into up till now. You have the capacity to be, to have, and to do virtually anything that you can put your mind to. But you must accept the responsibility of deciding exactly what it is you want and then dedicating yourself wholeheartedly to achieving it.

Here is an excellent thinking exercise for you: for the rest of your career, practice *zero-based thinking* in everything you do. Zero-based thinking requires that you draw a line under all of your decisions up till now and ask yourself this question: "Is there anything in my life that I am doing that, knowing what I now know, I wouldn't get into again today if I had it to do over again?"

In times of turbulence and rapid change like today, and for the rest of your life, you will always have at least one answer to that question. There will always be at least one thing that you are doing that, knowing what you now know, you wouldn't get into again if you had it to do over.

Get Serious About Your Future

You can't do very much about the current enormousness and ac-
celeration of change, but the one thing that you can do is get serious about yourself and your basic need for security and stability.
In no area is this more important than in the areas of job security
and financial freedom. You must especially focus on increasing
your ability to make a good living and provide for yourself in the
months and years ahead.

Above all, to position yourself for tomorrow you must think
continuously and seriously about your work today, your earning
ability, and the work that you will be doing one, three, and five
years from today. You must plan to achieve your own financial security, no matter what happens.

The engineer Charles Kettering once said, "I object to people running down the future. I am going to live all the rest of my
life there." One of the greatest mistakes that people can make,
and the one with the worst long-term consequences, is to think
only about the present and give no thought to what might happen
in the months and years ahead.

Multiple Jobs and Careers

When our grandfathers started work, it was quite common for
them to get a basic education and then go to work for a company
and stay with that same company for the rest of their working
lives. When our parents went to work, it was more common for
them to change jobs three or four times during their lifetimes,
although doing so was difficult and disruptive.

With increased turbulence and change in the national and global economies, a person starting work today can expect to have *six* full careers between the ages of twenty-one and sixty-five, and fourteen full-time jobs that last two years or more. A college graduate will have six different jobs by the age of thirty-five.

According to the Cato Institute, a prominent think tank, fully 40 percent of American employees in the twenty-first century will be "contingency" workers. This means that they will never work permanently for any single company. They will continue to move as needed, from company to company, from job to job, earning less money than full-time employees and accruing very few, if any, benefits in terms of health-care and pension plans.

Think Ahead Five Years

Imagine what your job will look like five years from today. Since knowledge in your field is probably doubling every two to five years, this means that 20 percent of your knowledge and skills are becoming obsolete each year. In five years, you will be doing a brand new job with brand new knowledge and skills. Ask yourself, "What parts of my knowledge, skills, and work are becoming obsolete? What am I doing today that is different from what I was doing one year ago and two years ago?"

What are you likely to be doing one, two, three, four, and five years from today? What knowledge and skills will you need and how will you acquire them? What is your plan for your financial future?

We are now in the *knowledge and communication age.* Today, the chief factors of production are knowledge and the ability to apply that knowledge to achieving results for other people. Your earning ability today is largely dependent upon your knowledge, your skill, and your ability to combine that knowledge and skill in such a way that you contribute value for which customers are going to pay.

Continual Learning

The solution to the dilemma of unavoidable change and restructuring is continual self-improvement. Your personal knowledge and your ability to apply it are your most valuable assets. To stay on top of your world, you must continually add to your knowledge and your skills. You must continually build up your mental assets if you want to enjoy a continual high return on your investment. And only by building on your current assets do you stop them from deteriorating.

By engaging in continual self-improvement, you can put yourself behind the wheel of your own life. By dedicating yourself to increasing your earning ability, you will automatically be engaging in the never-ending process of personal and professional development. By learning more, you prepare yourself to earn more. You position yourself for tomorrow by developing the knowledge and skills that you need to be a valuable and productive part of our economy, no matter which direction it goes.

Mental Cross-Training

You earn what you are worth, and you continually become more valuable, by learning the things you need to learn to get excellent results in your job.

World-class athletes have known for many years that the only way they can perform at their very peak is by developing all of their various muscles and abilities in a balanced way. In its simplest form, physical cross-training requires that you work on endurance, strength, and flexibility in a rotating format.

In mental cross-training, you must do the same thing with your repertoire of knowledge and skills. First of all, you need to determine the subjects that you have to be good at in order to be in the top 10 percent in your field. Your job is to make the decision, right now, to go all the way to the top. And the fortunate thing is that if anyone else has done it, you can do it as well. You simply need to follow in their tracks.

Key Result Areas

The process of your moving to the top of your field revolves around your identification of the Key Result Areas of your job. There are seldom more than five to seven skill areas that you absolutely, positively have to be good in to get to the top. There may be a hundred things you do in the course of your work, but there are basically only five to seven areas where you need to commit yourself to excellent performance in order to move way ahead of the rest of the field.

These Key Result Areas (KRAs) are where you begin your program of mental cross-training. If you are in sales, for example, your seven KRAs are: prospecting, getting appointments, establishing a relationship with the client, identifying the problem the client has that your product or service will solve, presenting your product or service as the solution, closing the sale, and getting re-sales and referrals. You will have to be absolutely, positively excellent in every one of these areas to be a great success in selling any product or service in any market.

Your Weakest Important Skill

Here is one of the most important discoveries about mental cross-training: if you are weak in any one critical area, that one area will set the height at which you use all your other skills. It will be the chief factor that determines your income and your level of success in your field. If you are absolutely excellent in six out of seven KRAs but you are weak in the seventh, that one weakness will hold you back from realizing your full potential in your job or position.

Let me give you an example. Let's say that you are absolutely excellent in every single aspect of selling except prospecting. Because of fear or negativity or competition in the marketplace, you are poor at getting appointments with new prospects who can, and will, buy your product or service. You may be outstanding at everything else, but if you can't get in front of people, you will ultimately fail.

In another example, let's say you are good at prospecting, and at getting appointments, and at establishing rapport, but when it comes to actually getting the client to take action or to closing the sale, you tense up, you are unable to do it, and you leave empty-handed. Again, you could be outstanding at everything except closing the sale and that alone will sabotage your entire career.

If you are in management, there will also be seven KRAs that determine how well you do your job, and the quality of results you get. They are planning, organizing, staffing, delegating, supervising, measuring, and reporting. If you are poor in any one of these seven areas, that could be sufficient in itself to hold you back from using all your other talents.

Assess Your Current Skill Level

If you are in sales, management, or any other field, here's an action strategy for assessing your current level of performance: First, identify your KRAs. Then give yourself a score from one to ten—with one being the lowest and ten being the highest—in each area. You will find that areas in which you have given yourself a low score are your primary areas of stress, frustration, anxiety, and underachievement in whatever it is you are doing. You need to have a score above seven in every key area for you to perform excellently in a well-balanced way.

It is essential that you be perfectly honest with yourself. It will do you no good to pretend that you are good at something when in reality your weakness is holding you back from achieving great success in your career.

Once you have determined the KRAs for your job and you have given yourself a score in each of the five to seven areas, take your score to someone who knows you, and ask him or her to score you. The best person for this is your boss, but a trusted coworker could do as well. You may be surprised at what they tell you.

Fortunately, all business skills are learnable. If you feel that you are not good at a particular skill, such as hiring or delegating, you can read books, listen to audio programs, and take additional courses. Sometimes a single learning experience will give you an essential skill that you can use for the rest of your career. Your goal is not necessarily to be the best in the business, but just to get your score above seven (out of ten) so that it doesn't hold you back.

Get a 360-Degree Analysis

One exercise that can help you, especially in management, is called the 360-Degree Analysis. In this process, managers are evaluated by all the people who report to them plus their superiors. Online questionnaires are sent out to everyone within that group, and each person is asked to evaluate the manager on a series of skills, abilities, and behaviors. Sometimes an outside consultant conducts in-person interviews instead, and the manager also conducts this same analysis on him- or herself. The consultant then summarizes the answers and presents them to the manager.

When this is done properly, it is extremely helpful to the person being analyzed. It often comes as a great shock to many managers that in some areas where they think they are quite strong, their coworkers and subordinates think they are quite weak.

For example, I had an executive working for me some years ago who felt that he was absolutely excellent at hiring people. He would not take any advice or input from anyone on the subject. He made his hires by the seat of his pants. And every single person he hired turned out to be a disaster. Eventually, he was forbidden to hire anyone.

His inability to learn how to properly interview and select the right people ultimately proved to be fatal in his career. He had to go back to working on his own because he was simply incapable of picking people to work with him, no matter what position he held.

Develop Your Key Skills

In mental cross-training, the areas where you are weak are usually the causes of the major problems in your career. They are the areas that preoccupy you and concern you the most. And they are often the activities where you get the worst results. You are most likely to become anxious when it comes to performing those activities. If you are not careful, you will start to avoid working in those very areas that can have the greatest possible impact on your overall results.

You might even practice denial, convincing yourself that you are already quite good in a particular area so you don't need to improve. This lack of realism is quite common and often results in career stagnation. This is why it is so important that you ask people around you to evaluate you in an objective way and tell you how well they think you are doing.

What Are Your Weakest Areas?

So, what are the areas that you need to work on to bring yourself up to a higher level of performance, to get better results? If you are not sure, have the courage and the honesty to go to other people and ask for their feedback. Remember, feedback is the breakfast of champions. You can't get better unless someone is willing to give you an honest critique and help you see yourself as you really are.

If you are in sales, it is absolutely essential that you get your sales manager or someone else to go out with you at least once a month for an entire day to evaluate your sales performance.

When this person comes along with you, he or she should sit quietly and say nothing, just watching the way you interact with the customer.

Afterward this person should tell you exactly what he or she saw, both the good and the bad. Unless you have this kind of honest feedback, it is impossible for you to improve. And instead of being defensive, make a decision to go to work on yourself and improve a weak skill area once you get some feedback, so that it is no longer a limitation on your performance.

Three Rules

There are three rules that I want to emphasize with regard to mental cross-training.

First: It doesn't matter where you are coming from; all that matters is where you are going. The future is more important than the past. You can't change the past, but you can change your future by changing what you do today.

Second: For your life to get better, *you* must get better. If you want to earn more, you must learn more. Knowledge is the chief source of value today. If you want to improve the quality of your life, you must improve the quality and quantity of your knowledge and skills.

Third: You can learn anything that you need to learn to become any person that you want to become, and to achieve any goal that you can possibly set for yourself. There are no limits except the limits that you set on your own mind.

From this day forward, make yourself into a "do-it-to-yourself" project. Begin and continue the lifelong process of getting better in all the areas that are important to you. Just as a champion athlete develops all of his or her muscles symmetrically and in balance, so you must develop your mental muscles in a balanced way as well. Mental cross-training is truly an important step toward gaining control of your destiny and earning what you are really worth.

The New Age of Competition

We are living in an economic age for which most people are largely unprepared. Massive shifts in economic activities and incredible dislocations of businesses and industries are taking place all over the country. Being either an employer or an employee today is like being a long-tailed cat in a room full of rocking chairs.

Your goal is to organize your life in such a way that you enjoy a good income, have a high standard of living, and are the master of your economic destiny rather than a victim of changing economic times.

Our Productivity Is Among the Highest

One critical edge the United States maintains is that we have one of the most productive workforces in the world. But there is a race on in this area, and we are in it. That's why, if you want to be employed at a good job for the indefinite future, you must get in and start competing as you have never done before.

Your job is an opportunity to contribute a value to your company in excess of your cost. In its simplest terms, your job is as secure as your ability to render value in excess of what it costs to keep you on the payroll.

If you want to earn more money at your current job, you have to increase your value, your contribution to the enterprise. If you want to get a new job, you have to find a way to contribute value to that enterprise. If you want any kind of job security, you must continually work at maintaining and increasing your value in a competitive marketplace. As Abraham Lincoln said, "The only security you can ever have is the ability to do your job uncommonly well."

Your Knowledge and Skill Are an Investment

And here's a key point: your education, knowledge, skills, and experience all are investments in your ability to contribute a value for which you can be paid. But they are like any other investments. They are highly speculative.

Once you have learned a subject or developed a skill, it is a sunk cost. It is time and money spent that you cannot get back. No employer in the marketplace has any obligation to pay you for your past skill and experience, unless he or she can use your skill to produce a product or service that people are ready to buy today.

Whatever job you are doing, you should be preparing for your next job. And the key questions are always: Where are the customers? What do people want to buy? Which businesses and industries are serving customers the best? Which businesses are growing in this economy, and which ones are declining?

I continually meet people who ask me how they can increase their income when their entire industry is shrinking. I tell them that there are jobs with futures and jobs without futures, and they need to get into a field that is expanding, not contracting.

There Are Always Lots of Jobs

There are three forms of unemployment in America: *voluntary*, *non-voluntary*, and *frictional*. Voluntary unemployment is when a person decides not to work for a certain period of time or not to accept a particular type of job, hoping that something better will come along. Non-voluntary unemployment is when a person is willing and able to work but cannot find a job anywhere. Frictional unemployment is the natural level; this includes the approximately 4 or 5 percent of the working population who are between jobs at any given time.

However, there are always jobs for the creative minority. You never have to be unemployed if you will do one of three things: first, you can change the work that you are offering to do; second, you can change the place where you are offering to work; or third, you can change the amount that you are asking for your services.

If there is no demand for your particular skills and experience, you will have to learn to do something else and provide skills that are in demand at the time. Employers don't care about your past. They care only about your future and your ability to contribute value to their customers.

You can also change your location. Sometimes you will have to move from one part of the country to another, from where there are few jobs to where there are more jobs. Many people transform their entire lives by moving from an area of high unemployment to an area of low unemployment. As they say, "Fish where the fish are."

Be Prepared to Work for Less

The third thing you can do to get back into the workforce is lower your demands. Remember, because your labor is a *commodity*, it is subject to the laws of supply and demand. If you ask too much, people will not hire you, because customers will not pay your demands in the price of the product or service that your organization produces. It is not the employer who is forcing this downward revision in wages; it is the customer, through his or her buying behavior.

There is a small, creative minority in the United States who are *never* unemployed. No matter what happens, they always have a job—sometimes two jobs. If they lose a particular position in one place, they find another position doing the same thing, or something else, somewhere else. They are fast on their feet. They move quickly, and they don't accept unemployment as an option. And they always have jobs. This must be your strategy as well.

There are always jobs to be done. Even in the worst economy, there are always problems to be solved and consumer needs to be met. For this reason all long-term unemployment is ultimately *voluntary*.

There are as many opportunities for you to fulfill your dreams and aspirations in the US economy today as there ever have been. There are thousands of jobs advertised in the newspapers and online every day—and even more that aren't advertised. You can be, have, or do anything that you can dream of by preparing yourself for better and better jobs. It is never crowded at the top. There are no traffic jams on the extra mile. Your goal must be to get good, get better, and then make yourself indispensable.

Double Your Income?

Would you like to double your income? When I ask this in my seminars, everyone raises his or her hand, nods his or her head, and usually shouts out, "Yes!"

I then go on to tell them that they are in luck. As an economist, I can assure them that everyone in the room is going to double his or her income—*if they live long enough.*

"The average income goes up at about 3 percent per annum," I observe. "Therefore, if you live and work for another twenty-two years, increasing your income at 3 percent per annum, with compound interest, you will double your income. Is that what you had in mind?"

Everyone then replies, "No!" Everyone wants to double his or her income much sooner than in twenty-two years. The good news is that there are people all around you who are increasing their income at rapid rates every year, and your goal should be to be one of them, rather than one of the 3 percenters.

Apply the 80/20 Rule

The 80/20 Rule, which is another name for the Pareto principle, is one of the most important and powerful of all time-management principles. This rule was discovered by the Italian economist Vilfredo Pareto. He divided society into two categories, the *vital few* and the *trivial many.* He found that the top 20 percent of people controlled 80 percent of the wealth. He later found that this law applied to work and business as well. It turns out that 20 percent of the things you do—the vital few—will account for fully 80 percent of the value of all of the work you do.

The *reverse* of this principle is that 80 percent of the things you do will account for 20 percent or less of the value of your activities. This 80/20 Rule applies to all aspects of business and personal life:

- Eighty percent of your sales will come from 20 percent of your customers.
- Eighty percent of your profits will come from 20 percent of your products.
- Eighty percent of your sales will come from 20 percent of your salespeople.
- Eighty percent of your income, contribution, and success will come from 20 percent of your activities.

If you make a list of ten tasks that you have to complete in a particular day, *two* of those items will turn out to be worth more than all the others put together. Your ability to identify and focus on the top 20 percent of tasks will determine your productivity and success as much as any other factor.

Increase Your Contribution

The law of three says that you must contribute $3 to $6 of profit, or even more, for every dollar that you wish to earn in salary. In terms of space, benefits, training, supervision, and investment in furniture, fixtures, and other resources, it costs a company approximately twice your basic salary to employ you. For a company to hire you, they have to make a *profit* on what they pay you. Therefore, you must contribute value greatly in excess of the amount you earn in order to stay employed. To put it another way, your contribution must be considerably greater than the amount you are receiving, or you will find yourself looking for another job, which many people are doing today.

To position yourself for tomorrow, here is one of the most important rules you will ever learn: the future belongs to the competent. The future belongs to those men and women who are very good at what they do, and getting better. As Pat Riley, in his book *The Winner Within*, wrote, "If you are not committed to getting better at what you are doing, you are bound to get worse." To phrase it another way, anything less than a commitment to excellent performance on your part is an unconscious acceptance of mediocrity.

It used to be that you needed to be excellent to rise above the competition in your industry. Today, you must be excellent even to keep your job for the long term.

The 80/20 Rule Again

The 80/20 Rule also holds true in terms of income and income growth. Eighty percent of the population increases their income at an average rate of 3 percent per annum. Since 3 percent per annum is the average rate of inflation, they never get ahead. They're always in debt. They never stop thinking and worrying about money. This lack of money hangs over their head like the Sword of Damocles, affecting their thinking, their relationships, their purchases, and almost everything they do.

Fortunately, people in the top 20 percent of earners increase their incomes by an average of 11 percent per year according to studies at the University of Chicago. People in the top 10 percent increase their incomes at an even faster rate. People in the top 5 percent increase their incomes faster still. Why is this?

The answer is simple. The people in the bottom 80 percent have largely flatlined. They have learned their jobs well enough not to be fired, and then they *have never gotten any better* at what they do. Ten years after starting in their particular fields, they are no better at their work than they were after one year. The tragedy is that this finding holds true for architects, engineers, doctors, lawyers, and other professionals, as well as for salespeople, managers, and employees at every level.

You have heard the story where the worker being laid off says, "How can you lay me off? I've got twenty years' experience."

"No," the boss says. "You have one year's experience, twenty times over."

You Can Only Coast Downhill

The sad fact is that the great majority of people living in our affluent society have been coasting for years. Now the chickens have come home to roost. Now it is no longer possible to get and keep a job, and increase your income, by just showing up. To be successful today, as they say in sports, you've got to suit up and get onto the field, determined to play hard and win. No one is entitled to a job anymore. And if you don't perform well, you will be cut from the team faster than ever before.

Use Compound Interest in Your Favor

If your income goes up by 11 percent per annum, you will double your income in six and a half years. And in six and a half years more, you'll double it again. And again. And again. Soon you will be living in a lovely house in a beautiful neighborhood, driving an expensive car and sending your kids to private school. Because of the law of compound interest, if your income keeps increasing, every element of your financial and personal life will improve at the same rate.

If your income increases at 25 percent per annum, which is not impossible, you will double your income even faster, every two years and seven months. If you keep doing the same things that enabled you to double your income over and over, you will double it again in another two years and seven months. By the miracle of *compounding*, you will soon be wealthy.

I have worked with salespeople and business owners who learned what you are going to learn in this book and went from earning less than $20,000 per year to more than $1 million a year in income in less than ten years. Compound interest and compound growth can be your best friends.

Action Exercises:

1. Identify the Key Result Areas of your job, the five to seven tasks that you absolutely, positively need to do well to get the results that you have been hired to get.

2. Give three answers to the question, "Why am I on the pay-roll?" Answer in terms of specific, measurable results that are required of you.

3. Determine your weakest important skill, the one that sets the height of your success and your income. Resolve to go to work on developing that skill today.

4. Think on paper. Make a list of everything you could start doing immediately to become more competent and valu-able at your job.

5. List the three changes you or anyone could make to get a job in any market. How do these apply to you?

6. Project forward five years and determine the skills you will need at that time to earn twice as much as you are earning today.

7. Be prepared to invest an average of two hours per day back into your becoming better at the most important things you do that determine your income.

CHAPTER FOUR

Capitalize on Your Strengths

One's only security in life comes from doing something uncommonly well.

—ABRAHAM LINCOLN

You have special talents and abilities that you can maximize to earn far more than you are earning today. Your goal is to identify those things that you can do in an excellent fashion and then commit yourself wholeheartedly to becoming the best in that part of your chosen field.

One of the qualities of superior men and women is that they are extremely *self-reliant.* They accept complete responsibility for themselves and everything that happens to them. They look to themselves as the source of their successes and as the main cause of their problems and difficulties. High achievers say, "If it's to be, it's up to me."

When they are not satisfied with something in their work, they ask themselves, "What is it in me that is causing this problem?"

They refuse to make excuses or blame other people. Instead, they look for ways to overcome obstacles and make progress.

Because they have this attitude of self-employment, they take a strategic approach to their work.

Think Strategically About Your Career

The essential element in strategic planning for a corporation or a business entity is the concept of return on equity. All business planning is aimed at organizing and reorganizing the resources of the business in such a way as to increase the financial returns to the business owners. It is to increase the quantity of output relative to the quantity of input. It is to focus on areas of high profitability and return and, simultaneously, to withdraw re-sources from areas of low profitability and return.

Companies that plan and act strategically in a rapidly changing environment are the ones that survive and prosper. Companies that fail to engage in this form of strategic thinking are those that fall behind and often disappear.

Increase Your Return on Energy

To achieve everything you are capable of achieving as a person, you also must become a skilled strategic planner in your life and work. But instead of aiming to increase your return on equity, your goal is to increase your return on *energy*.

Most people in America start off in life with little more than their ability to work and generate income. More than 80 percent of millionaires in America are self-made. They started with nothing at all. Most of them have been broke, or nearly broke, several times during their lifetimes. Most fortunes began with the sale of personal services. But the people who eventually get ahead are those who think and do certain things in specific ways, and those actions set them apart from the average.

Perhaps the most important approach top people take, consciously or unconsciously, is to look at themselves strategically. They think about themselves as a bundle of resources, capable of doing many different jobs. They carefully consider how they can best utilize their special combination of knowledge and skills in the marketplace and how they can best capitalize on their strengths and abilities to increase their returns to themselves and their families.

Your Marketable Skills

One of your greatest responsibilities in life, to yourself and to your family, is to identify, develop, and maintain one or more important marketable skills. Your job is to become very good at doing something for which there is a strong market demand.

In corporate strategy, we call this the development of a *competitive advantage.* For a company, a competitive advantage is defined as an area of excellence in producing a product or service that gives the company a distinct edge over its competition. This *area of excellence* enables a company to sell more of its products and services at higher prices with less buyer resistance.

In capitalizing on your strengths as the president of your own personal service corporation, you also must have a clear competitive advantage. You also must have an area of excellence. You must do something that makes you different from, and better than, your competitors—those people who want to earn the money you want to earn by doing what you are doing.

Your Competitive Advantage

Your ability to identify and develop this competitive advantage is the most important strategy you implement in the world of work. It's the key to maintaining and increasing your earning ability. It's the foundation of your financial success. Without it you're simply a pawn in a rapidly changing environment. But with a distinct competitive advantage based on your strengths and abilities, you can write your own ticket. You can take charge of your own life. You can always get a job. And the more distinct your competitive advantage, the more money you can earn and the more places at which you can earn it.

There are four keys to the strategic marketing of yourself and your services. These are applicable to huge companies such as General Motors, to candidates running for election, and to individuals who want to earn the very most money in their careers.

Think Strategically About Your Career

The first of these four keys is *specialization*. This is essential today. No one can be all things to all people. A jack-of-all-trades also is a master of none. That career path usually leads to a dead end. Specialization is the key. Men and women who are successful have a series of general skills, but they also have one or two *core skills* at which they have developed the ability to perform in an outstanding manner and do excellent work.

Your decision about how, where, when, and why you are going to specialize in a particular part of your job or career is perhaps the most important decision you will ever make in your career. It was well said by strategic planner Michael Kami that "Those who do not think about the future cannot have one."

The major reason why so many people are finding their jobs eliminated and themselves left unemployed for long periods of time is that they didn't look down the road of life far enough and prepare themselves well enough for the time when their current jobs would expire. They suddenly found themselves out of gas on a lonely road, facing a long walk back to regular and well-paying employment. Don't let this happen to you.

Look into Yourself

In determining your area of specialization, put your current job aside for the moment and take the time to look deeply into yourself. Analyze yourself from every point of view. Rise above yourself and look at your lifetime of activities and accomplishments.

It may be that you are doing exactly the right job for you at this moment. You might already be capitalizing on all your strengths. Your current work might be ideally suited to your likes and dislikes, to your skills and temperament, and to your personality. Nevertheless, you owe it to yourself to be continually expanding the scope of your vision and looking toward the future to see where you might want to be going in the months and years ahead. Remember, the best way to predict the future is to *create* it.

You Are Remarkable

Your special talents and abilities make you unique, different from anyone else who has ever lived. Your remarkable combination of education, experience, knowledge, problems, successes, difficulties, and challenges, and your way of looking at and reacting to life, make you *extraordinary*. You already have within you potential competencies and attributes that can enable you to accomplish virtually anything you want in life.

Even if you lived for another hundred years, it would not be enough time for you to plumb the full depths of your potential. You will never be able to use more than a small part of your inborn abilities. Your main job is to decide which of your talents you're going to exploit and develop to their highest and best possible use right now.

What is *your* area of specialization? What are you especially good at right now? If things continue as they are, on your current growth track, what are you likely to be good at in the future—say one, or two, or even five years from now? Is this a marketable skill with a growing demand? Or is your field changing in such a way that you are going to have to change as well if you want to keep up with it?

Looking into the future, in what area should you specialize if you want to rise to the top of your field, make an excellent living, and take complete control of your financial future?

Becoming a Copywriter

When I was twenty-two, unemployed and insecure, I answered an advertisement for a position as copywriter for an advertising agency. As it happened, I had failed high-school English. I really had no idea what a copywriter did. I still remember the advertising executive who interviewed me and how nice he was about pointing out that I wasn't at all qualified for the job.

But something happened inside me in the course of the interview process. The more I thought about it, the more I thought how much I would like to write for advertising. Having been turned down flat during my first interview, I decided to learn more about the field.

I went to the city library and began to check out and read books on advertising and copywriting. Over the next six months, while I worked in a department store, I spent every evening and weekend studying them. As my knowledge grew, I applied for copywriting jobs at advertising agencies in the city. I started with the small agencies first. When they turned me down, I asked them *why* they didn't want to hire me. What was wrong with my application? What did I need to learn more about? What books would they recommend? And to this day, I remember that virtually everyone I spoke with was helpful to me and gave me good advice.

By the end of six months, I had read every book on advertising and copywriting in the library and applied to every agency in the city, working up from the smallest agency to the very largest. By the time I had reached that level, I was ready. I was offered jobs as a junior copywriter by both the number one and the number two agencies in the country. I took the job with the number one agency and within six months I was writing advertising copy for large multinational corporations.

You Can Learn Anything You Need to Learn

The point of this story is that you can learn almost anything you need to know to master and then excel at almost any job. You must simply decide what skill you need and apply yourself to *learn what you need to learn.* This is such an obvious strategy for higher income and greater success that most people miss it completely.

Some years after becoming a copywriter, I decided that I wanted to get into real-estate development. I had heard of several people who had built homes and commercial properties, including friends of mine from high school, and they had made a lot of money. I decided that that would be a good way for me to make money as well. Using the same strategy that had served me so well in copywriting, I went to the city library and began checking out book after book on real-estate development. At the time I had no money, no contacts, and no knowledge of the industry. But I knew the great secret: I could learn what I needed to learn to be successful in any field that I committed myself to.

Starting With Nothing

Within six months, I had tied up a piece of property with a $100 deposit and a thirty-day option. I put together a proposal for a shopping center, got tentative commitments from two major anchor tenants and several minor tenants that together took up 85 percent of the square footage I had proposed.

Then I sold 75 percent of the entire package to a major development company in exchange for the company's putting up all the cash and providing me with the resources and people I needed to manage the construction of the shopping center and the completion of the leasing. Virtually everything that I did I had learned from books written by real-estate experts—books on the shelves of the local library.

As you might have noticed, the fields of copywriting and real-estate development are very different. But these experiences, and all the other business situations I have been in over the years, had one element in common: success in each area was based on two decisions—first, to specialize in that area, and second, to become extremely knowledgeable in that area so that I could do a good job.

Your Success in the Past

In looking at your current and past experiences to select an area of specialization, one of the most important questions to ask yourself is what activities have been most responsible for my success in life to date?

How did you get from where you were to where you are today? What talents and abilities seemed to come easily to you? What tasks do you do well that seem to be difficult for most other people? What sort of work do you most enjoy doing? What activities do you find most intrinsically motivating?

In capitalizing on your strengths, your level of interest in and excitement and enthusiasm about the particular job or activity is a key factor. You'll always do best and make the most money in a field that you really enjoy. It will be an area that you like to think about, and talk about, and read about, and learn about. Successful people love what they do, and they can hardly wait to get to it each day. Doing their work makes them happy, and the happier they are, the more enthusiastically they do their work, and the better they do it as well.

How Are You Different and Better?

The second key to marketing yourself strategically is *differentiation*. You must decide what you're going to do to be not only different but also better than your competitors in the field you choose. Remember, you only have to be good in *one* specific area to move ahead of the pack. And you must decide what that area should be.

Your area of differentiation is the work you do in an excellent fashion. You do it better than 90 percent of the people in your field. What is your area of excellence today? What *could* it be if you decided to become excellent at a new skill? What *should* it be if you want to get to the top of your field and be one of the highest-paid people in your industry?

What is the most important and valued skill in your business, the one that most contributes to financial results? The greater the impact you can have on sales and profitability, the more valuable you become, and the more money you will earn.

Segment Your Market

The third strategic principle in capitalizing on your strengths is *segmentation*. You have to look at the marketplace and determine where you can best apply yourself, with your unique talents and abilities, to earn the highest possible return on energy expended.

What customers, companies, and markets can best utilize your special talents and offer you the most in terms of financial rewards and opportunities?

One employer or industry can place an average or lower than average value on your special talents and abilities, while another type of business can value your skill so highly that they will pay you a lot for the results you can get.

Once I made a living as a door-to-door salesman, cold-calling on businesses and businesspeople, selling a $20 product and earning an $8 commission on each sale. Then I was offered another job also in selling and based on cold-calling, this time selling mutual funds and other investments that cost thousands of dollars. By using the same skill set I had developed in door-to-door sales, I was soon earning thousands of dollars a month. My whole life changed. How could this experience translate to your skills and the opportunities around you?

Concentrate Your Efforts

The final key to personal strategic marketing is *concentration*. Once you have decided on the area in which you are going to specialize, and how you are going to differentiate yourself, and in what segment of the marketplace you can best apply your strengths, your final job is to concentrate all of your energies on becoming excellent in your specific area and doing an exceptional job. The marketplace only pays extraordinary rewards for extraordinary performance.

In the final analysis, everything that you have done up to now is simply the groundwork for becoming outstanding in your chosen field. When you become very good at doing what people want and need, you begin moving rapidly into the top ranks of the highest-paid people in our society.

Action Exercises:
1. Identify the three most important and valuable things you do in your work, those activities that have the greatest impact on your income.
2. Determine your area of excellence. Identify the parts of your work where you perform in the top 10 percent in your field.
3. Identify which skills have been most responsible for your greatest successes in your career.
4. Decide what it is that you most love to do in your work. How could you structure your time so that you are doing this more of the time?
5. Identify your competitive advantage, the area of skill or ability where you are superior to others in your field. If you don't yet have one, what could it be? What should it be? What is your plan to achieve it?
6. Segment your market. In what areas could you earn far more by using your special skills at a higher level?
7. See yourself as a bundle of resources. What could you do to earn the highest return on energy in today's economy?

CHAPTER FIVE

Get the Right Job

Opportunity often comes disguised in the form of
misfortune, or temporary defeat.

—NAPOLEON HILL

To earn what you are really worth, you have to be in the right
job in the first place. Sometimes you could earn more just by
walking across the street and getting a new job if your special talents and skills could be used to get more valuable results for a
different employer.

This is a challenging time in human history to be out in the job
market and working to survive and thrive. However, in spite of
problems in the economy, there are countless opportunities and
possibilities for talented people to find or create great jobs and earn
more than they ever have before. In spite of the Great Recession,
more than 90 percent of the workforce in the United States is employed, making money, and moving ahead with their lives. The rate
of new business formation has passed more than one million new

companies per year. A large number of employers are looking for talented, committed people to help their businesses grow. There are millions of job openings advertised every month.

The biggest single limit on business success today is the ability to attract and keep good people, like you. More people are becoming financially successful today as a result of doing an excellent job and being paid well for it than ever before. Your job is to participate fully in the new economy and to realize your true income potential by getting and keeping an excellent job and then moving upward and onward in your career for the rest of your working life.

A World of Experience

Personally, I have worked in twenty-two different companies and industries. I have worked my way up into the position of chief operating officer of a $265-million company. In my various positions, I have hired numerous people for a variety of jobs in a variety of industries. In addition, I have worked as a consultant, trainer, and advisor to more than a thousand corporations throughout the United States and Canada and worldwide. In doing so, I have consulted and advised extensively on hiring practices and given insights and ideas to many executives that have enabled them to select the ideal people for their organizations.

Over the years, I have trained many thousands of men and women on the subject of "Creative Job Search" and taught them how to get good jobs, get better jobs, get paid more, and get positioned better for rapid advancement. Almost every graduate of my Creative Job Search programs went on to find a new or better job within days of completing the seminar.

In this chapter, I will give you some of the very best ideas, strategies, methods, and techniques ever discovered for getting a great job that pays well in any economy. By applying these ideas and methods, you will put your career onto the fast track.

Take Control of Your Career

This is the starting point of career success and maybe the most important point of all. Most people wander out into the job market, go on interviews, and then accept the best job that is offered to them. But this is not for you. Your goal is to take complete charge of your career from this moment forward.

Remember, with the rapid change that now characterizes the workplace, the average person starting work today will have fourteen full-time jobs lasting two years or more and as many as six full careers over the course of his or her working lifetime. To weather these storms of lifelong career change, you must be proactive, not reactive. You must take complete control of your career and guide yourself into those industries and jobs that can give you the very best pay and the greatest opportunities for the future.

Develop Your Options

Remember, you are only as free as your *options*. The more skilled you become at getting the job you want, the more money you will make and the more choices you will have. The more you know about how to get the job you want, the easier it will be for you to move upward and onward with each step of your career.

Most people start their job search by answering Internet or newspaper ads, sending out résumés or using employment services of some kind. But the fact is that 85 percent of all jobs available in your community, right now, are not advertised. They do not appear anywhere. They are not posted on any employee bulletin board, nor are they to be seen in the newspapers. They are hidden and waiting for you to discover them, like buried treasure.

A self-directed job search enables you to take control of your career and your life. It puts you behind the wheel. It makes you the architect of your own destiny. It gives you a sense of control and develops a positive mental attitude. It ensures that you will never be unemployed.

See Yourself as Self-Employed

As I've said, to take control of your career is to begin to view yourself as *self-employed*. See yourself as the president of a company with one employee: yourself. See yourself as having one product that you sell in a competitive marketplace: your personal services. See yourself as 100 percent responsible for your life and for everything that happens to you.

As I wrote earlier, you are the president of your own personal service corporation. Every day, every week, and every month, you go into the marketplace and you sell the services of your own corporation to the highest bidder.

As president of your own personal service corporation, you are completely responsible for marketing and selling yourself and for presenting yourself in the marketplace in the most attractive way. You are responsible for production—for producing the highest quality and quantity of services of which you are capable. You are responsible for quality control—for doing excellent work at whatever is entrusted to you. You are responsible for research and development—for continually upgrading your knowledge and skills so that you can do your job better and faster. You are responsible for finance—for organizing your financial life in such a way that you accomplish your financial goals. You are the president of your own company.

This attitude is the starting point of getting the job you want, not only in the short term, but for the rest of your career.

Analyze Yourself Carefully

Before you go out and look for a job, you must sit down and take stock of yourself. You must look deeply into yourself and make some clear decisions about who you are and where you want to be in the future. It is only when you have a good understanding of yourself and your own desires and ambitions that you can go out and get the job you want.

Remember the famous observation by Socrates: "The unexamined life is not worth living."

Look into yourself and identify your most marketable skills. Look into yourself and make a list of all the things that you can do that someone in the marketplace would be willing to pay for. Here are some questions that you can ask and answer before you ever go to your first interview:

1. What are your skills? What can you do well? What have you learned through education or experience that enables you to make a valuable contribution to an employer?
2. What have you done well at various jobs and in activities in the past? What sorts of activities have been most responsible for your success in your work life today?
3. What sort of activities in your work and your personal life do you most enjoy? Remember, you will almost always be most successful doing the things that you enjoy the most.
4. What parts of your work do you perform most easily? What you've done well at in the past is often an indicator of what you would do best at in the future.

Doctors say that accurate diagnosis is half the cure. In your case, accurate self-analysis—taking the time to sit and think through the answers to these questions—is half the work of getting the ideal job or position.

Where you have been happy and successful in the past is the very best indication of where your true talents and abilities lie for the future. Your goal is to find a job doing something that enables you to use the very best and highest qualities and talents that you have inside.

Decide Exactly What You Want

Most people go into the workplace and take whatever is offered to them. They allow the employer to determine the direction of their careers. That's because many people have never really given much thought to their careers since they took their first job. They have merely reacted to the demands placed upon them as the years went by. But this is not for you.

Here is a series of exercises that you can practice throughout your career to make sure that you are on the right track:

First, describe your *ideal job*. Imagine that you could have any job in the world. Exactly what would that job be? Remember, you can't hit a target that you can't see.

Second, look around you in the marketplace. If you could have any job doing anything, what *exactly* would it be? If you do see a job that you like, go and talk to somebody who is doing that job, and ask for their advice. You'll be amazed at the insights that people will offer you in just a few minutes of conversation.

Third, project yourself into the *future*. What sort of work would you like to be doing in three to five years? Everyone has to start at the beginning with a new job or career, but you must be clear about where you want to be in your career in the future. This enables you to make a much better decision when taking a particular job in the first place.

Fourth, consider, if you could work anywhere in the country, taking into consideration weather and geography, *where* exactly you would like to work. It is amazing how many people pack up and move to a different part of the country before taking a new job because that is where they have always wanted to live. Could this be true for you?

Fifth, ask yourself what *size* and *type* of company you would like to work for. Would you like to work for a small, medium-sized, or large company? Would you like to work for a high-tech or low-tech company? Would you like to work for a service or a manufacturing company? Describe your ideal company in as much detail as you possibly can.

Sixth, think about what kind of *people* you would like to work with. Describe your ideal boss. Describe your ideal colleagues. Remember, the quality of the people and your social relationships at work are going to have more impact on your happiness and success than any other factor. Choose your boss and your colleagues with care.

Seventh, determine how much you would like to *earn*. How much do you want to be earning in one year? Two years? Five years? This is very important. You should be asking questions about your earning ability and the earnings ceiling at the job interview. Be sure that the job is in a company or situation that enables you to achieve your earnings goals within the time horizon you've projected.

Eighth, ask *who else* is working at the kind of job that you would like to have, or earning the kind of money that you would like to earn. What are they doing differently from you? What qualifications do they have that you still need to acquire?

Ninth, find out whom you know who can *help you* position yourself for the kind of job you want. Who can give you advice? Who can point you in the right direction? Whom should you ask for help? Remember, everyone who succeeds does so with the help of other people.

Tenth, ask yourself what *level of responsibility* you desire. How high up do you want to rise in your career? What title or position would you be most comfortable with?

The most amazing thing is this: the more specific and clear you are about exactly what it is you want to do, where you want to do it, and how much you want to earn, the easier it is for someone to hire you and pay you the kind of money you want to make. Go back over these questions and answer them one by one before you go out looking for the job you want.

Think About the Future

One of the characteristics of leaders, as shown in more than 3,300 studies, is that they have *vision*. This is a quality that you can develop by simply deciding to do so. You develop vision by projecting five or ten years into the future and thinking about how you would like your life to be, if everything were ideal in every respect.

This is called back-from-the-future thinking. Take out a piece of paper and imagine that five years have passed. Write out a description of what your career would look like if it were perfect in every way. Create a clear vision of your ideal job, company, and work environment. Write out how much you would be earning, what you would be doing, the kind of people you would be working with, and the level of responsibility you would have achieved.

Start Where You Are

Once you have a clear vision, come back to the present and ask yourself, "What would I have to do *today* to begin making my five-year vision a reality?"

Leaders continually create a clear ideal for themselves and then look for ways to make that ideal a reality. When you develop a clear vision for yourself and your future, the only question you then ask is, "How can I make this vision come true?"

How can you go about finding or creating the kind of job that you want, where you can achieve your full potential? When you are clear about your vision for yourself and your future, you will be amazed at how much more likely you are to find the real job you want.

Understand the Job Market

There are certain rules and principles of work and employment. Some of these are practical and some are economic. They are all basically facts of life. They are principles that you have to take into consideration for as long as you work for a living.

The basic rule is this: your rewards in life, both tangible and intangible, will always be determined by the value of your *service* to other people. Your income will be determined by what you do and how well you do it, and by the difficulty of replacing you. Your income security can only be guaranteed when you do something that is important, something for which there is a demand in the marketplace, something in which you are difficult to replace.

Your Labor Is a Commodity

A second fact of economic life is that your labor, whatever you do, is viewed and treated as a *commodity* in the marketplace. It is seen as a factor of production. Your effort is viewed as a certain quantity and quality of labor of a specific kind that can be applied to produce certain quantities of products or services. That's why all labor, including your own, is subject to the economic law of supply and demand.

A change in technology, or in market preferences by consumers, or in the economy, can make a particular skill obsolete almost overnight. A person who on Friday is fully employed and working twelve hours a day can find him- or herself out of work on Monday because of this kind of rapid change.

Employers Are Customers

Here is another important economic fact that you must understand: *employers are customers.* They want the very most for the very least when they go shopping for employees.

When you go into the marketplace to sell your services, you attempt to get the very most money for what you have to offer. When employers go into the marketplace to purchase your services, they attempt to get the very most services for the very least amount of money.

And here's the point: *everybody works on commission!* In a free society such as ours, everyone who works for a private business is on commission. Everyone receives a percentage of the sales of the organization. No matter where you are in the organization, your salary or wage represents a part of the sales revenue generated by the company. And where there are no sales, there are no paychecks.

For this reason, jobs are not determined so much by what you want as by *what other people want.* The work you do is not determined so much by your background, your knowledge, your skills, or your ability as by what people need, what people want, and what people are willing to pay for.

You must be continually adjusting your offerings, your talents and skills, your work and effort, so that they are in conformity with what people want, need, and are willing to pay for. This is the key to understanding the job market.

The Universal Hiring Rule

This is the great principle that gives you complete control over your career. The universal hiring rule simply says that wherever you can find an opportunity to increase revenues or reduce costs by an amount greater than the cost of hiring you, you can actually create your own job.

The laws of business economics state that an employer will continue to hire people so long as each additional person contributes more in dollar value to the company than he or she costs in salary to the company. This means that you are surrounded with opportunities to create the kind of job you want by simply finding ways to contribute more in value than you represent in cost. Your salary is ultimately determined by the financial impact that you have on your employer.

The 80/20 Rule Revisited

The Pareto principle can be applied today to the things that you do or can do for a company. Twenty percent of your activities will account for 80 percent of the value of your contribution to your employer. In fact, your ability to identify the most important things you can do to contribute value to an employer is the critical determinant of how fast you get the job you want, how much you get paid, and how rapidly you get promoted.

You have many different talents and abilities. Your responsibility is to think through the few things among those you can do that represent the highest and best use of your time for an employer. Sometimes, your ability to do a single specific task in an excellent fashion can make you one of the most valuable and highly paid people in the organization. Whenever you interview for a job or think about different jobs, you must continually analyze the job in terms of the most critical and valuable parts of it that you can do in an excellent fashion.

One of the most important questions you must ask each day is "How can I add more value to this particular job or position?"

When you have a job, or even before you get a job, you should be asking about and determining your highest-value-added activities. And the clearer you can make your financial contribution to a prospective employer, the more rapidly he or she can hire you and put you to work.

The Universal Hiring Rule is also the universal rule for getting ahead in your career.

Fish Where the Fish Are

There are thousands of jobs available at any time, in any economy, no matter what the economic situation. Even in times of high unemployment, more than 90 percent of people are working and earning good money. Anyone who is really serious about getting and keeping a job can do so. There are few limitations.

For example, every individual company, large or small, is a separate job market. There are approximately 50,000 companies per one million people in the United States. Some of these companies are large and employ thousands of people. Most of them are small. But the fact remains that there is approximately one company, or one job market, for every fourteen people in America.

In addition, every department in every company is a job market unto itself. Every department is like a small business. It has revenues and expenses. It has functions it must perform and responsibilities it must discharge. Every department hires and fires, advances and promotes, deploys and utilizes different forms of labor.

Every individual in every department in every company who has the authority to hire people is a job market. Even in a company with as few as twenty people, there are four or five individuals who have the authority to hire others. Each of these four or five people is a job market unto him- or herself, with specific requirements, with problems unsolved and needs unmet.

Jobs, Jobs Everywhere

This means that in every city or town, in every economy, there are literally thousands of companies, departments, or individuals who are job markets and who have varying levels of needs for specific services. Your job is to find the right one.

Remember, a job is merely a problem that is not yet solved. It is an opportunity to render useful service, to help someone overcome an obstacle or achieve a goal. Whenever you find a person with a problem or an opportunity, full- or part-time, you can create your own job. Read the newspapers and magazines looking for job openings.

Check the Internet regularly. Register on every website where potential employers post job openings, such as www.craigslist.com, www.careerbuilder.com, or www.monster.com. Speak to placement agencies and executive recruiters. Cast a wide net. And always remember, there are vastly more jobs available than there will ever be talented people to take them.

Use Your Time Well

When you start looking for a job, you must accept complete responsibility for using every minute of every day in the very best way possible. You should look upon the job search as a full-time job, taking forty to fifty hours each week, starting first thing in the morning and continuing all day long.

The more active you are, the more people you see, the more information you acquire, and the more opportunities you investigate, the more likely it is that you are going to get a far better job than a person who waits at home for someone to call or who goes out on an occasional job interview.

You are the president of your own company. As the president, you are responsible for every aspect of your company's operations. You are responsible for planning, for organizing, for setting priorities, for delegating, for self-supervision, and, especially, for getting results.

Define Your Ideal Job

You start your job search by answering the questions I gave you earlier, in writing. You then write out a description of your ideal job, in every respect. You determine what you want to do, where you want to do it, and how much you want to earn. You determine what kind of people you want to work for and what size of an organization you want to work in. You determine your values and your vision for your ideal future. Then you go to work.

Plan Your Day In Advance

Get up each morning and plan each day in advance. Make a list of everything you have to do that day, and organize the list by priority. Select the most important item on the list, and begin with it immediately. All day long, work from your list, and challenge yourself to get through everything as quickly as you possibly can.

Arise early, exactly as if you were already fully employed. Get up, get dressed, and get ready to go exactly as if you were going to work.

Eat a light, high-energy breakfast. Go to the table or desk that you have set aside as a workplace for your job search and get on the telephone or the computer. Make your first call or send your first email by 8:30 a.m. Whenever possible, schedule your first face-to-face appointment for early morning, even before normal working hours.

Getting up, getting dressed, and looking good not only increase your self-confidence and improve your attitude, but also positively impress other people, both in your own home and outside it.

Remember, you should never see yourself as unemployed. You are a fully employed person who is merely in a *temporary* state of transition.

Ask yourself the key question, "What is the most valuable use of my time right now?" Whatever the answer to that question is, be sure that you are working on it every single minute.

The most important question to continually ask yourself in getting the job you want is, "Is what I am doing *right now* leading to a job interview or a job?" Do not drop off your dry cleaning, pick up your laundry, read the newspaper, watch television, or chat with your friends. See yourself as fully employed at getting a position where you are fully employed. Don't waste time. Develop a sense of urgency. Move quickly. Cover as much ground as you possibly can every single day.

Keep Good Notes

A key time-management principle for a job search is to *keep accurate notes* of every conversation and every discussion. Write everything down. Get yourself a spiral notebook that you carry with you everywhere. Write down everything that is talked about and every detail that you learn. At the end of a given event's notes draw a line under the section, and begin with the next set of notes. You can then refer back to conversations that you had even weeks ago, and you will always have a written record.

Do Your Homework

When you are looking for the job you want, you engage in the same activities that a sales professional would. The three activities essential to sales success are prospecting, presenting, and following up.

Your job is to *prospect* thoroughly and develop the greatest number of leads that you possibly can. Then, you meet with and make *presentations* to as many prospective employers as possible. Third, you *follow up* with the very best opportunities until you get the job you want.

One of the most important keys to success in selling today is what is called *pre-call research.* Do your homework. Find out everything that you possibly can about the individual, the organization, and the industry before you call on anyone the first time.

Fortunately, with the Internet you can do more and better research in a few minutes than has ever before been possible in human history. And you cannot imagine how impressive it is when a job candidate calls on a person with a file full of information on that individual and his or her organization and industry. It gives you a critical edge in the final decision. This critical edge can open a door for you that can change the entire direction of your life.

Prepare Thoroughly In Advance

In selling, the difference between the amateur and the professional is summarized in what is called *pre-call planning.*

This means that you take a few minutes beforehand to develop your plan for an interview. You review all the information you have on this industry, this organization, and this person. You develop a series of questions that you want to ask. You review what is going on in the industry and both the levels of employment and the types of incomes that are possible. You read the newspapers, and you check the Internet to find out what competitors are doing and offering.

Preparation is the mark of the professional. It is absolutely amazing to me the number of people who have applied to me for jobs who have no idea what my company does. They somehow think that they are such good talkers that they can get away with fast talk and use fakery to cover up the fact that they have not spent any time preparing for the interview. Don't let this happen to you.

Put yourself in the position of the employer and think through what he or she will need to know in order to offer you the kind of job that you really want. The better prepared you are, the more impressive you will appear, and the easier it will be for someone to hire you.

Sow Seeds Everywhere

As I have said, fully 85 percent of the jobs available in your market are not advertised or publicized anywhere. This is called the hidden job market.

Perhaps the most important part of the hidden job market today lies on the Internet. Up from virtually nothing a few years ago, approximately one-fourth of all jobs are now filled through Internet placement advertising.

You should not only surf the Internet job sites regularly but you should also make sure that your qualifications and interests are on every job site that might be visited by employers who are looking for someone like you.

Internet Job Search

Getting a job on the Internet is not easy. It is a skill that you must learn through practice. You start by visiting the main Internet job sites that you see advertised all around you. If you don't know where to start, go to a search engine such as www.craigslist.com, www.aol.com, or www.bing.com and go to the employment section. Examine the various job categories and then read the descriptions of the jobs that are being offered.

Get as much information as you possibly can about the various job sites. Some Internet job sites specialize in one kind of employee, and some specialize in another. Some are local, and some are national. When you list on an Internet job site, your résumé and your information become instantly available to potential employers nationwide.

There are many opportunities for you to post a brief description of your abilities and the job you are looking for at no charge. Some sites will charge you a placement fee, but these are usually worth it because they are much more aggressive in tracking potential employers to the site. Remember, you always get what you pay for in life.

There are also job fairs held in every community every year. These are advertised in the newspaper and on the radio. You should visit these job fairs and talk to the various employers exhibiting there. Find out what they are looking for today and what they will be looking for in the future. Even if you are currently employed, keep sowing seeds everywhere you go so that you can create a rich harvest of employment in the future.

The more seeds you sow, the more likely you are to get the job you really want.

Increase Your Probabilities of Success

Your success in getting a great job is a numbers game. It is based on the law of averages. It is based on probabilities. This simply means that the more people you see and talk to, the greater the probability that you will be in the right place at the right time, with the right person and the right opportunity, to get the job you want.

To increase the likelihood of getting a good job, read the newspapers in your city carefully. Especially, you should study the business and career sections. Read with a red pen or a high-lighter in hand, and make careful notes for follow-up. Make it a point to be aware of the trends in business in the city in which you wish to work.

Knowledge Is Power

Read the trade publications, and check the Internet sites in your field or in the field in which you want to work. You can subscribe to these, buy them at your local magazine stand, read them on-line, or find them at your local library. When you begin inter-viewing and asking around for a job, ask people what magazines or publications are written for that particular field. When you read these magazines, look for stories concerning companies that are growing, expanding, or engaging in innovative activities.

Remember, heightened business activity creates the demand for new people.

Read all the business magazines, both local and national, keeping an eye out for stories about companies and trends in the industry in which you wish to work. Read the local business journal from cover to cover, and look for the companies that are announcing new positions or introducing new products or services. Business journals usually contain information on jobs that are available, as well as people who are moving up within their existing companies.

Look for the Names of Decision-Makers

Look for the names of key people in various companies and departments of companies. Especially look for the names of those who have been recently promoted. People who have been recently promoted often make immediate staff changes and create job opportunities for people who call.

Look for active, growing organizations that are announcing a new expansion or increased profitability. These companies are always looking for more good people. They offer lots of opportunities and they pay well.

Look for new product releases and the introductions of new services. Wherever a company is expanding its products or services, there are job opportunities to sell the product, distribute the product, service the product, install the product, and handle the administration and details associated with the product.

Whenever you see a company that is expanding and an executive who has been promoted, phone the company immediately, and tell the person you talk to that you are looking for a job in that industry and that this company is of interest to you. Ask the receptionist for the name of the person you should speak to. Arrange to go in and see the person and interview for a job.

It is absolutely amazing how many great job opportunities you can uncover by simply taking action on the news and information all around you about the business and industry that you want to work in.

The Three Cs to Getting Any Job

There are three Cs to getting the kind of job you want and earning the kind of money you want to earn. These three Cs basically remain constant throughout your working career. They are contacts, credibility, and competence.

First, the more *contacts* you have in the marketplace, the more likely it is you will find the job you want. The more people you know and who know you, the more likely it is you will uncover one of the 85 percent or more of job openings that are never listed anywhere.

This is why it is so important for you to *network continually.* Join clubs and associations. Ask people for referrals and references. Tell your friends, relatives, and associates that you are in the market for a new job. Make sure that everyone you know is aware that you are available and looking for a job.

Nothing is more important than your circle of contacts. The great majority of jobs that are filled in the hidden job market are filled because someone knows someone. And you can expand your range of contacts just by telling people that you are available and asking for their help and their advice.

Your Reputation Is Important

The second C is *credibility*. This is made up of your reputation and your character. Your credibility is the most important single quality about you in terms of getting recommendations and referrals from your contacts.

Make sure that everything you do is consistent with the highest ethical standards. Make sure that you never say or do anything that could be misconstrued by anyone as anything other than excellent conduct and behavior.

Remember, people will only recommend you for a job opening if they are completely confident that they will not end up looking foolish as a result of something you do or say.

Be Good at What You Do

The third C is *competence.* In the final analysis it is how good you are and how good you have been in your previous jobs that will determine, more than anything else, how good you can be at the job under consideration. Next to your character, your level of competence will be the single most important factor in determining your success in your career. This is why you must be continually working to maintain and upgrade your levels of competence through personal study all your working life.

The Seven Qualities Most in Demand

Every employer has had a certain amount of experience with both good and bad employees. For this reason every employer has a pretty good idea of what he or she wants more of. Here are the big seven:

1. The first quality that employers look for is *intelligence.* In every study, it has been found that fully 76 percent of the productivity and contribution of an employee will be determined by his or her level of intelligence. Intelligence in this sense means the ability to plan, to organize, to set priorities, to solve problems, and to get the job done. Intelligence refers to your level of common sense and your practical ability to deal with the day-to-day challenges of the job. The key to demonstrating your intelligence is for you to *ask intelligent questions.* One of the hallmarks of intelligence that is immediately evident is curiosity. The more you ask good questions and listen to the answers, the smarter you appear.

2. The second quality sought by employers is *leadership ability.* Leadership is the willingness and the desire to accept responsibility for results. It's the ability to take charge, to volunteer for assignments, and to accept accountability for achieving the required results of those assignments.

   The mark of the leader is that he or she does not make excuses. You demonstrate your willingness to be a leader in the organization by offering to take charge of achieving company goals and then committing yourself to performing at high levels.

3. *Integrity* is the third quality sought by employers. It's probably the most important single quality for long-term success in life and at work. Integrity begins by being true

to yourself. This means that you are perfectly honest with yourself and in your relationships with others. You are willing to admit your strengths and weaknesses. You are willing to admit where you have made mistakes in the past. Especially, you demonstrate *loyalty*. You never say anything negative about a previous employer or a person whom you have worked with or for. Even if you were fired from a previous job, never say anything negative or critical.

4. The fourth quality that employers look for is *likability*. Employers like people who are warm, friendly, easygoing, and cooperative with others. Employers are looking for people who can join the team and be part of the work family.

   Men and women with good personalities are invariably more popular and more effective at whatever they do. *Teamwork* is the key to business success. Your experience in working as part of a team in the past and your willingness to work as part of a team in the future can be among te most attractive things about you in applying for a job.

5. *Competence* is the fifth quality sought by employers. We spoke about this earlier. Competence is terribly important to your success. It is really the foundation of everything that happens to you in your career.

   In its simplest terms, competence is *the ability to get the job done*. It is the ability to set priorities, to separate the relevant from the irrelevant tasks, and then to concentrate single-mindedly until the job is complete.

6. *Courage* is the sixth quality that employers look for. This is the willingness to take risks. Courage also means the willingness to accept challenges, the willingness to take on big jobs or even new jobs where there is a high degree of uncertainty and the possibility of failure.

Courage also means the willingness to speak up and say exactly what you think and feel in a difficult situation. Employers admire men and women who are not afraid to speak their minds. And you demonstrate this in a job interview when you ask frank and direct questions about the company, the position, and the future that you might have with the organization.

7. The final quality employers look for is *inner strength.* Inner strength means that you have the determination and the ability to persevere in the face of adversity. Inner strength means that you have the quality of *persistence* when the going gets rough. You demonstrate inner strength when you remain calm, cool, and relaxed during the job interview. If you are calm and cool during the interview, it is a good indication that you will be calm and cool in the inevitable crises that occur during the day-to-day operations of the company.

Above all, it is your *character*, which is the sum total of all your positive qualities, that will have the greatest impact on whether you get the job you want. Your job now is to continue working on your character by practicing the behaviors of top people at every opportunity.

Write Résumés That Get Results

Your résumé is a combination *sales-and-promotion tool.* Just as a company produces brochures and promotional materials for products and services, your résumé is your promotional tool for yourself. It is advertising yourself as a "product" who can perform specific functions and get certain results.

As an advertising piece, your résumé must be interesting, inviting, factual, attractive, and upbeat; it must entice the reader to want to meet you, talk to you, and learn more about how you can perhaps help achieve his or her goals.

The fact is that it often requires *hundreds* of résumés to get a single job offer. Very few people are ever hired simply because of a résumé. It is like a business card. Many people are actually hired without their résumé ever being read in the first place.

The ideal length of a résumé is *one page*, with a maximum of two pages. People today are extremely busy, and they don't have time to read long documents. Therefore make your résumé short and to the point.

Two Types of Résumés

There are two types of résumés: *chronological* and *functional.* The chronological résumé is based on your dates of employment. It lists your previous jobs with the most recent at the start, going back month by month and year by year and describing your work experience and education from the beginning of your adult life.

You use a chronological résumé when you've had a career path that shows consistent growth and development. A chronological résumé is best when you started with a simple job and then moved up gradually to more and more complex jobs.

The Functional Résumé

A functional résumé, on the other hand, is organized by job function or achievements. Very often you will use a functional résumé when you have spent a good deal of time with a single company but have performed a variety of different tasks within that company.

In a functional résumé, you identify the various job functions or titles that you have had. You then list your accomplishments and achievements in each of these job areas. For example, if you started with a company and worked up from a lower position to a higher position, you would start off by listing your title in the highest position and the things you accomplished. You would then list your title in the second position and the things you accomplished in that job.

Transferability of Results

The most important part of a résumé or a job interview is called *transferability of results.* What employers are looking for is proof that you have already achieved the same results that they would like someone to achieve in the position they are interviewing for. Your job is to convince the employer that you, as the result of your previous education and experience, are the ideal person to achieve the results that the employer desires.

Ideally your résumé should be *left behind* after you have had a personal interview with the employer. Whenever possible, avoid mailing your résumé in advance. If, however, you are responding to an advertisement and you have no choice but to mail your résumé, always send it with a *cover letter* that refers specifically to the advertisement and to the job that you are seeking. Even if your letter is handwritten, you should send it as a covering letter with the résumé.

Finally, once you have either sent your résumé or left your résumé behind, be sure to *phone back* in a couple of days to find out their reaction. Don't be afraid to be persistent, so long as you are polite. Persistence in seeking a position is considered a positive attribute by an employer.

Informational Interviewing

Informational interviewing is the key to a *creative* job search. When you interview for hire, you are the interviewee. You sit there and the prospective employer asks you questions and grills you about your background and ability.

However, in informational interviewing you are the *interviewer.* You have control over the interview. You are actually screening the employer rather than being screened by the employer. You can ask hard questions about the business and the industry without worrying about whether or not you make a good impression.

Some form of informational interviewing is used by virtually everyone who gets a good job with high wages in a short period of time. It is one of the most powerful job-seeking techniques ever discovered, and it will work for you if you practice it.

You begin by making a list of prospective companies that you would like to work for. You then identify one of these and gather information about both the company and the person in the company whom you want to talk to. Telephone the receptionist and say you are a potential customer. Ask him or her to send you a complete package of promotional literature on the company and its products and services. Study its website carefully.

Getting the Interview

You then phone and ask for an appointment with the right person. You tell that person, by phone, voice mail, email, or letter, that you would like to interview him or her to get some ideas about working in this particular field.

You use these words: "I'm doing some research into this industry. I'm thinking of making a career change into this field, and I am talking to several authorities in the industry to get some information and ideas on how to make the best choice."

Surprisingly enough, people who are normally too busy to talk to you, or who do not have the time for interviews, will actually make time to give advice to someone who is looking to move into and up in an industry where they work.

You tell the prospective employer, "I would like to interview you for about ten minutes and ask you some specific questions." People usually love to be interviewed. And if you talk for only ten minutes, you will almost invariably get an appointment within a few days.

Interview Like a Professional

You are now the interviewer. Before you go to the interview, create a list of questions about the industry and the company. Ask about the prospects for the future, the prospects for different people in different jobs, and so on. Make very careful notes during your interview. At the end of ten minutes, be prepared to thank the individual and depart. Often, you will be invited to stay longer.

Never accept a job offer during the informational interview. If the employer asks you if you are looking for a job, you respond by saying, "No, not at this time. I am still in the process of doing my research, and I'm not far enough along to make that kind of a decision."

After the interview, immediately go home and write a *thank-you note*. This is a powerful part of the informational process, and it virtually guarantees your ability to go back at a later time with your findings.

Ace the Interview

There are several things that you can do to make each interview as successful as it can possibly be. Each of these steps has an impact on helping you to get the kind of job you really want:

1. Always be *punctual*. Allow yourself enough time to get there, taking the address and the traffic into consideration. As a general rule, employers are advised never to hire a person who arrives late for a job interview.

2. *Dress well* for the job interview. Your clothes can account for 95 percent of the first impression you make on your prospective employer, because first impressions are almost always visual.

   Dress the way you would expect to dress for the job for which you are applying. Many people are hired for no other reason than that they were the best-dressed of the candidates interviewed.

   Many otherwise excellent men and women are disqualified by the employer at the first meeting because they did not dress well for the job interview.

3. Before going into the interview, take a few moments to *breathe deeply* and relax your shoulders. Breathing deeply six or seven times will actually release endorphins in your brain and give you a sense of well-being and calmness.

   Close your eyes for a few moments and *visualize yourself* as calm, confident, and relaxed. Create a clear mental picture of yourself as smiling, positive, and completely in control of yourself and your emotions during the interview.

4. When you meet the interviewer, *smile* and shake hands firmly. Look the person directly in the eye and say, "How do you do?" A good handshake is full and firm, where you grasp the entire hand and squeeze in a firm but non-aggressive way. Both men and women should give a full-palm handshake when they meet a person for the first time.

5. Interview the interviewer. Most interviewers start off with a series of questions that are aimed at drawing you out

and getting a better idea of who you are. You should take control of the interview by asking questions about the company, the industry, and the kind of person that the interviewer is looking for.

The more questions you ask and the more you help to uncover the real needs of the prospective employer, the more likely it is that the prospective employer will see you as being the kind of person who can fulfill those needs.

Sell Yourself Professionally

The job interview is really a sales call. You are in *sales* when you are looking for a job. You are going out to sell yourself to someone else. The type of job you get and the type of salary you command will be a measure of how well you have sold yourself at this critical point in your career.

Many people don't like the idea of selling. They don't like to see themselves as salespeople. Unfortunately, this is the type of attitude that leads to underachievement in life. The fact is that everyone who wants to sell his or her ideas or services to others is a salesperson. The only question is whether or not you are any good at it.

Uncover the Needs of the Employer

Every employer has needs that are not yet satisfied. Every employer has problems that are not yet solved. Every employer represents an opportunity for you. In many cases, employers will actually create jobs for people who convince them that they can help satisfy needs and solve problems.

Your prospective employer has only *one question* in mind when interviewing you for a job. It is the same question that every customer asks when considering whether or not to buy a product or service. And your employer is a customer. You are the product or service that is for sale. And your prospective customer's question is, "What's in it for me?"

Your prospective employer wants to know, "How will I personally benefit from hiring you?" He or she wants to know, "What can you do for me specifically?" And finally, your prospective employer wants to know, "How can I be sure that what you say is true?"

Prove What You Say Is True

Your aim in the job interview is to demonstrate that you can *achieve, avoid,* or *preserve* something for your employer. You and the employer must be absolutely clear about what it is you are offering to achieve, avoid, or preserve.

The way that you impress the prospective employer in a job interview is by focusing on the employer's needs and problems. And the way you do this is by asking good questions. There is a direct relationship between your ability to ask good questions and listen carefully to the answers and the speed at which you get the job you want.

Your key goal in a job interview is to convince the employer that you can achieve a result that he or she needs, or improve a situation that he or she is facing, below the cost of hiring you. The better you plan and prepare, the better you will be at convincing the employer that you are the ideal person for this job.

Getting the Job

You have done your research and your informational interviewing. You have met with the prospective employer and you have sent your follow-up thank-you letter. You have researched the company and the industry, and you have taken complete control of your career. You have decided where you want to work and who you want to work for. You are now ready to close the sale.

Perhaps the most powerful tool of all in a job interview is called self-selection. Your intense desire for the job, demonstrated by everything you say or do, is extremely impressive and influential in getting you the job you want.

When you are closing the sale for the job you want, your goal is to convince the employer overwhelmingly that this is the right job for you and that you are the right person for this job. Describe your experience as it relates to the position. Describe what you feel you could do for the employer.

Focus on Contribution

Explain the *contribution* you feel you could make to the prospective employer and to the company. Don't be afraid to be enthusiastic and assertive in selling yourself to the prospective employer.

Be active, direct, and straightforward in the interview. Smile, nod, and make it clear that you are fully involved in the discussion. Show that you are really eager to get this job with this company and this person.

Especially, *tell* the prospective employer that you really want this job. Sometimes, this is impressive enough to cause the person to hire you rather than someone else.

There is probably nothing that you can say that is more impressive to a prospective employer than the words "I really want this job. If you give me a chance, I promise you I will do a terrific job. You won't be sorry."

Remember, emotions are contagious, and employers are as susceptible as anyone. Your excitement and enthusiasm for a job can have an impact on the employer's decision that is greater than all the résumés you ever write. Your success in persuading the employer that you are the right person will determine the quality of the job you get and the salary that goes with that job, as much as or more than any other factor.

Negotiating the Best Salary

You have now interviewed and successfully persuaded the employer that he or she should hire you for the job. Next comes the issue of salary negotiation. What you do at this point can have a major impact on your income, your lifestyle, and your future. Follow these instructions carefully.

First, you should have a good idea of *how much* you want to earn as a salary for this position. You should have done your research and spoken to other people. You should know what the salary range is for a position of this kind. You should never go in blind, having no idea of how much money to ask for.

If you are not sure, phone an executive recruitment agency or a personnel placement agency and ask to speak to one of their account representatives. Tell him or her who you are and what kind of job you are interviewing for. Ask what salary range makes sense for this particular job. They will almost always try to help you out if you ask politely.

Neither Accept Nor Reject the First Offer

Whatever is offered to you, never accept either the job or the salary the very first time it comes up. Always ask for time to think it over, even if you want this job very badly. Use the twenty-four hour rule. Always ask for twenty-four hours to think about a job offer before you accept it. The more you ask for time to think it over, the better the job and job benefits you are going to get when you make the final decision.

When an employer offers you a salary, he or she usually has a salary range in mind. The salary range is usually 20 percent above and below the average amount paid for that position. For example, if a position pays roughly $2,000 per month, the employer will be thinking in the range of $1,600 (20 percent below) to $2,400 (20 percent above) per month.

The employer will make every effort to hire you at the *lowest possible amount* that you will accept. Your job, on the other hand, is to aim for the very highest amount that the employer is prepared to pay. Your goal is to ask for an amount at the top of the salary range in the employer's mind.

Increase the Bracket

Here is how you do it: When an employer offers you a salary of $2,000, for example, you should suggest a figure that is between 110 percent and 130 percent of that amount. This is called *bracketing*. If the suggested figure is $2,000, you should say that you feel that excellent performance in this position would be worth between $2,200 and $2,600. You raise the limits of the bracket in the employer's mind and in the conversation.

Surprisingly enough, the employer will often settle for an amount that is midway between the two figures that you propose—in this example, an amount of $2,400. This is the upper end of his or her salary range and is usually more than he or she planned to pay, but he or she will often give it to you if you ask for it in this way.

In some cases, you will have to settle for a lower salary to start. When this happens, you immediately ask what you will have to do to get an increase in salary. Be specific, and ask the employer to put it in writing in his or her letter of acceptance to you.

Negotiate for Benefits

If you cannot get a higher salary, you can negotiate for the benefits that come with the job. You can negotiate for a longer vacation, more days off, and more sick days.

You can also ask for additional perks that go with the position, such as an office, a car, an expense account, and other things.

In any case, whatever salary, benefits, and package you negotiate, immediately ask if you can get an increase within ninety days if you do a good job. Your power to negotiate for a better package at a higher salary later is greater at the moment of taking the job than it ever will be again.

Be sure to take lots of time to think through and discuss all the details involved in the job. Be sure to ask for clarity and have everything that you have agreed to written down on paper. You will then be ready to put your career onto the fast track.

All the Key Ideas

There are hundreds of books and articles on the subject of job searches. Nonetheless, what you have learned in this chapter covers the most important ideas ever discovered to help you earn what you are really worth.

The thought that you put into your career and into the job you get will have as much of an impact on your life as any other decision you ever make or series of actions you take. It is vitally important that you become absolutely excellent at creative job searching and that you review and practice these ideas over and over again until they become habits that you practice for the rest of your life.

Getting the kind of job you want is both an art and a science. It is a learnable skill that you can develop by reading this chapter over and over again and then taking action on what you have learned. There are no limits to what you can accomplish.

Action Exercises:

1. Imagine that you could have any job, earning the kind of money you want to earn, anywhere in the country. What would it be?

2. Determine the three most important skills you have that enable you to make a valuable contribution. What are they?

3. Ask who else is doing the kind of work you are doing and earning the kind of money you want to earn. What are they doing differently?

4. Determine the kind of results that you can get for an employer that he or she would gladly pay you well for.

5. Decide upon the additional skills and abilities you need to learn and develop to get the job you really want.

6. Project forward five years and imagine that your work and income are perfect at that time. What are you doing and how much are you earning?

7. Choose one action that you are going to take immediately to get and keep the ideal job for you.

CHAPTER SIX

The Future Belongs to the Competent

The big secret of life is that there is no big secret. Whatever your goal, you can get there if you're willing to work.

—OPRAH WINFREY

We are living today in the most advanced age of humankind. It has seldom been possible to live better or longer than people live right now, and if anything, it is only going to get better in the years ahead.

You are extraordinary. There never has been and there never will be anyone in the world with the same unique combination of talents, abilities, knowledge, experience, insights, desires, goals, and ambitions that you have. The odds of there being two people just like you are more than 50 billion to one, which is another way of saying that it will never happen.

At birth a baby's brain contains 100 billion neurons. Each cell in your brain is connected to as many as 20,000 other cells by dendrites and ganglia. The popular psychologist Tony Buzan has estimated that 100 billion neurons taken to the 20,000th power means that the number of thoughts your brain can create is greater than the number of all the molecules in the known universe. The amount would be equivalent to the number one followed by ten pages of zeros. In a single day, you think about 70,000 thoughts with little effort or concentration.

The Smarter You Get, the Smarter You Get

The wonderful thing about your incredible mind is that it is like a muscle. The more you use it, the stronger and more flexible it becomes. Unfortunately, the opposite is also true. If you don't use it, you lose it. Without constant exercising and stretching, your brain becomes weaker and soon loses much of its alertness and speed.

Keeping this in mind, think about the fact that, whatever you are earning, you should be earning twice as much as you are right now. The only question you should be asking is, "Why aren't I *already* earning that amount?"

When I ask my audiences this question in seminars, they immediately start to think of all the reasons why they aren't already earning twice as much. And what I have found over the years is that most of those reasons are merely *excuses*. They are "limiting beliefs" that hold people back. These excuses usually have no substance, no foundation in reality. They are merely reasons for earning less than the excuse-maker is worth, ideas that he or she has accepted, usually unthinkingly, and learned to live with.

Starting from Behind

When I started off my adult life, I had few advantages. I had dropped out of high school and worked at laboring jobs for several years before I got into sales. In sales I spun my wheels for many months, barely earning enough to survive and pay for my room in a small boarding house.

Then one day, I began asking, "Why is it that some people are more successful than others?"

I noticed that there were people all around me, including people younger than I was, people who also had limited educations and had come from poor backgrounds, who seemed to be doing better than I was. They were earning more money, driving better cars (where I had no car at all), and wearing nicer clothes. In the evenings they went to restaurants and nightclubs, and on the weekends they went to beautiful resorts and took nice vacations. This mystified me. Why were some people doing so well, while the rest of us were struggling?

The Great Question

Then I did something that changed my life. I went to the most successful man in my company, a sales guy who was earning ten times as much as anyone else in our business, and I asked him why he was more successful than I was. What was he doing differently from what all the other salespeople and I were doing?

He quite willingly offered to help. He first asked me to explain to him how I was selling, how I was approaching prospects and what I was saying. I told him. He explained to me that I was doing it all *wrong*. He then told me how to open a sales conversation, develop rapport with the prospect, ask good questions, and talk about my product intelligently. He explained that selling, like any other field, is made up of a definite series of steps—a process—and that if you follow them, you will make more sales than if you don't.

Do What Top People Do

So I did what he told me to. I went out and began asking more questions and focusing on building rapport and trust with prospects. I took the time to learn about their situations and needs relative to what I was selling. I began to match my products with their specified needs, answer their questions or concerns, and ask them to buy my product. And they did. And my sales and my income went up and up.

Within a year, my income had doubled and then tripled. Soon, I was teaching people who had never sold anything before the same professional selling process that I had learned. And their incomes went up and up as well. Today, many years later, many of those salespeople are millionaires and multi-millionaires, owning and operating multiple businesses.

The Iron Law of the Universe

What I learned was the law of cause and effect. This law says that for every *effect* there is a *cause*. If you can identify the effect that you desire, you can trace it back to a cause. If you then duplicate the cause, you will soon get the effect you want.

In other words, if you do what other successful, highly paid people do, you will soon get the same results they do and become a successful and highly paid person yourself. There is no mystery.

The great challenge is that the world is full of people who are doing what *failures* do and being continually amazed when they find that they get the same results that failures get. They are implementing the same causes and getting the same effects. This is happening *by law*, not by chance.

Nature is neutral. Nature doesn't care. Whatever you put in, you get out. If you fail to put it in, you fail to get it out. The best part of the law of cause and effect is that, whatever goal you can set for yourself, or whatever success you desire, if you simply do what other people have done before to achieve the same result, you can, within reason, have it as well.

Change Your Mind-Set

What is the difference between people in the bottom 80 percent and people in the top 20 percent? Simple. People in the top 20 percent have a different mind-set from people in the bottom 80 percent. Not only do the words that they use have different meanings, but their thinking styles are different as well. Top people are in "constant learning mode." They are curious, interested, and eager to absorb new knowledge. They are hungry to learn. They read, listen to audio programs, attend seminars, and ask questions of people who know more than they do.

They are great listeners. They take notes in every seminar and conversation.

The people in the top 20 percent see that there is a direct link between new information and increased income. They never stop improving. They know that one of the best time-management tools in the world is to get better at what you do. Geoffrey Colvin, author of the bestselling *Talent Is Overrated*, refers to this as "deliberate practice."

The people who get ahead faster than others are those who take the time and put in the hard work to deliberately learn and practice new, essential skills that can help them to advance up the ladder of their careers. They never stop learning and growing. Their entire focus is to push to the front.

The Only Real Difference

In its simplest terms, the difference between people at the bottom of the ladder and people at the top is practical knowledge and skill. The people who are ahead today, and getting further ahead, are those who have the knowledge and skill that they require to excel in their fields, and they are continually adding to that knowledge and skill.

Just as money grows with compound interest, knowledge and skills also grow with the compounding effect. Each bit of valuable information that you learn turns part of your mind into Velcro, enabling you to recognize and hook onto other pieces of information that can help you in that area. Your mind becomes like a burr that catches bits of information and ideas that can be helpful to you in doing your job even better than before.

The Power of Persuasion

For you to earn what you are really worth, you must become not only more and more valuable to your company but more persuasive and influential as well.

Fully 85 percent of what you accomplish in your career and in your personal life will be determined by how well you get your message across to others, and by how capable you are of inspiring people to take action on your ideas and recommendations.

You can be limited in other areas, lacking education, contacts, and intelligence, but if you can interact effectively with others, and get them to cooperate with you, your future can be unlimited.

There is a series of ideas, techniques, and skills that you can use to accelerate your progress toward becoming a powerful communicator. But first, there are two major myths about communication that must be dispelled.

Myths About Communicating

The first myth, which many people believe, is that if a person can *talk*, he or she can communicate with others. Men especially, according to the research, think that by speaking louder and faster, they are being more effective in dealing with people. Many people think that because they have the gift of gab, because they have no problem talking to others on any subject that comes to mind, they are good communicators.

Often, exactly the opposite is true. Many people who talk a lot are poor communicators, even terrible communicators. Many people in sales and business think that being able to string a lot of words together in a breathless fashion makes them excellent at sending a message that is understood by others. However, in many cases, people who do this are seen as difficult to follow, boring, or obnoxious.

Let me state again: *the ability to talk is not the same as the ability to communicate.* The ability to communicate is the ability both to send and to receive a message. The ability to communicate is the ability to make an impact on the thoughts, feelings, and actions of someone. Many people who consider themselves excellent talkers are not very effective at all in this regard.

The ability to talk to one or more persons is only the most basic requirement for communication. It's the starting point, the jumping-off place. Effective communication is something else again.

Communicating as a Natural Skill

The second myth about effective communication is that it's a skill that people are or are not born with. Either you have it or you don't, goes the myth. If you're not extroverted, gregarious, and outgoing, you don't have what it takes to be a good communicator.

Again, nothing could be further from the truth. Communication is a skill that you can learn. It's like riding a bicycle or typing. It takes time and practice, over and over. But if you're willing to work at it, you can rapidly improve the quality of every part of your relationships with others, as you will soon see.

The Communication Process

Communication is a process that requires both a sender and a receiver. This process of communication can happen between two people, or between a speaker and a group. The same process of interaction takes place whenever two or more people exchange ideas.

First, the sender thinks of an idea or image that he or she wishes to convey to the receiver. The sender then translates the idea or image into words, either written or spoken. Those words constitute the basic message that is transmitted to the receiver. The receiver catches the words, like a baseball player catches a baseball, and then translates them into the ideas and pictures that they represent in order to understand the message.

The receiver then acknowledges receipt, and replies by translating his or her own ideas and pictures into words and transmitting them back to the sender. When the message has been sent and the receiver has acknowledged receiving it by transmitting a response that the sender then receives, accepts, and understands, the communication is complete.

Communication Is Complicated

If this sounds complicated, it is. Probably 95 percent of all the difficulties among human beings, and within organizations, are caused by breakdowns in the communication process. Either the senders do not say what they mean clearly enough, or the receivers do not receive the message in the form in which it was intended.

An enormous number of factors can interfere with any communication, and every one of these factors can lead to a *distortion* of the message in some way. Probably every problem you'll ever have will be somehow associated with a failure or breakdown in the communication process.

According to Albert Mehrabian, a communications specialist, there are three elements in any direct, face-to-face communication: *words*, *tone of voice*, and *body language*. You've probably heard that words account for 7 percent of the message, tone of voice accounts for 38 percent of the message, and body language accounts for fully 55 percent of the message.

For an effective communication to take place, all three parts of the message must be *congruent*. If there is any incongruence, the receiver will be confused and will tend to accept the predominant form of communication rather than simply the literal meaning of the words.

The Total Message

Your choice of words is important, but the better you can coordinate all three of the ingredients of communication, the more impact your message will have, and the greater will be the likelihood that a person will both understand it and react the way you want them to.

Sometimes, you will say something that you feel is innocent or noncontroversial to a person, and he or she will be offended. When you try to explain that the words you used were inoffensive, the person will tell you that it was not the words; it was your tone of voice.

The third ingredient of communication, body language, is also important. The way you sit or stand or incline your head or move your eyes relative to the person with whom you're communicating will have an enormous effect on the message received.

For example, you can increase the effect of your communication dramatically by leaning toward the person you're speaking to. If you're sitting down, this is easy. If you're standing up, you can accomplish the same effect by shifting your weight forward onto the balls of your feet toward the person you're talking to. When you make direct eye- and face-contact with the person, and combine this with focused attention, you *double* the impact of your words.

One of the easiest ways for you to break off a conversation, in an effect almost like knocking a needle off a phonograph record, is just to turn away from a person and look into the distance when he or she is speaking. That will usually cause the person to stop speaking, and feel that he or she has just been abandoned in the middle of the conversation.

Become an Excellent Listener

You've heard the saying that "God gave you two ears and one mouth, and in conversation you should use them in those proportions." Truer words were never spoken. The best communicators are excellent *listeners*. The worst communicators are continuous talkers. They allow no pauses or silences in the conversation.

Often the most important part of your message is the part conveyed by the pauses you make between thoughts and ideas. The message is conveyed in the silence during the lulls. All master communicators have learned to be comfortable with silence.

As the ground can absorb only a certain amount of water, so a person can absorb only a certain amount of information. If you pour too much water onto the ground, the water will form into puddles instead of soaking in. Information in a person's mind is very much the same. If you don't give someone an opportunity to absorb what you're saying, by pausing and waiting quietly and patiently, he or she will be overwhelmed by the continuous stream of thoughts and ideas and often will misunderstand the message and miss the point.

Preparation Ensures Better Understanding

One of the most vital requirements for effective communication, especially with important messages, is preparation. Preparation is the mark of the true professional. The late coach Paul "Bear" Bryant of the University of Alabama football team was famous for saying, "It's not the will to win but the will to prepare to win that counts." In all communications, the will to prepare in advance of talking and interacting with people is the key to achieving maximum effectiveness.

In high-school and college debating, where individuals and teams are judged on their ability to get their ideas across effectively and carry their points, the debaters are taught to prepare exhaustively. Especially, they're taught to prepare the debate from the point of view of their opponents before they prepare their own arguments.

Lawyers also are taught to do this in law school. Before they go into court, lawyers think through every possible piece of evidence or information that favors the opposing side. They then prepare their arguments in such a way as to undermine what they think the opposing side will present as its strongest point.

What Are His or Her Motivations?

The more important the communication, either in business or in personal life, the more important it is to prepare for it. As you do so, remember that people do things for their own reasons, not for yours. Everyone's favorite radio station is WIIFM, "What's in it for me?"

So think through where the other person is coming from. What is his or her point of view? What are his or her problems or concerns? What is he or she trying to accomplish? What is his or her level of knowledge or information about the subject under discussion?

The best communicators do not use a lot of words, but they choose their words carefully, in advance. People appreciate straight talking. Avoid the tendency to dress up your message and sugarcoat it. When you have a question or a concern or when you want something, come right out and say it without confusion or distortion. You'll be amazed at how much better you will feel and how much more positively someone will respond to your message.

Ask Your Way to Success

In getting your point across, perhaps the most important word of all is *ask*. The most effective people are those who are the best at asking rather than talking. They ask questions to uncover real needs and concerns. They ask questions to illuminate objections and problems that people might have with what they're suggesting. They ask questions to expand the conversation and to increase their understanding of where people are really coming from.

You get your message understood by getting out of yourself, putting your ego aside, and focusing all of your attention on the other person. You get people to do the things you want them to do by presenting your arguments in terms of their interests, in terms of what they want to be, and have, and do. You prepare thoroughly in advance of any important conversation. You think before you speak, and you think on paper. You can say almost anything if you say it, or ask it, pleasantly, positively, and with courtesy and friendliness.

The ability to communicate is a skill that you can learn by becoming genuinely interested in people and by putting their needs ahead of your own when sending a message or asking them to do something for you. When you concentrate your attention on building trust, on the one hand, and seeking to understand, on the other, you'll become known and respected as an effective communicator everywhere you go.

Action Exercises:
1. Identify the most successful people in your field and determine what it is that they are doing differently from you.
2. Decide today that you are going to double your income in the next year or two, and then determine what results you will have to achieve to do it.
3. Go to the top people in your field and ask them for advice about what you could do to be more successful faster; whatever they tell you, do it immediately.

4. Resolve today to prepare thoroughly for every meeting and presentation that can affect your career.
5. Take a course in public speaking so you can be more persuasive in selling your ideas to others.
6. Listen carefully and attentively to people when they speak. Don't interrupt.
7. Ask questions to find out what people really want and listen to the answers.

CHAPTER SEVEN

Double Your Productivity

In the end it is important to remember that we cannot become what we need to be by remaining what we are.

—MAX DEPREE

What you are about to learn in this chapter can change your life. These ideas, methods, and techniques can increase your efficiency and effectiveness, boost your productivity, double your income, lower your stress levels, and make you one of the most productive and valuable people in your business or field today. They are the *indispensable* keys to your earning what you are really worth.

All successful, highly paid people are very *productive*. They work longer hours, and they put more into each hour. They get a lot more done than the average person. They get paid more and promoted faster. They are highly respected and esteemed by everyone around them. They become leaders and role models.

Inevitably, they rise to the top of their fields and to the top of their income ranges, and so can you.

Every single one of these tested and proven strategies for managing your time and doubling your productivity is learnable through practice and repetition. Each of these methods, if you practice it regularly, will eventually become a habit of both thinking and working.

When you begin applying these techniques to your work and to your life, your self-esteem, self-confidence, self-respect, and sense of personal pride will go up immediately. The payoff for you will be tremendous and will last the rest of your life.

Make a Decision!

Every positive change in your life begins with a clear, unequivocal decision that you are going to either do something or stop doing something. Significant change only begins for you when you decide to either get in or get out, either fish or cut bait.

Decisiveness is one of the most important qualities of successful and happy men and women, and decisiveness is developed through practice and repetition, over and over again until it becomes as natural to you as breathing in and breathing out. The sad fact is that people are poor because they have not yet decided to be rich. People are overweight and unfit because they have not yet decided to be thin and fit. People are inefficient time wasters because they haven't yet decided to be highly productive in everything they do.

Decide today that you are going to become an expert in time management and personal productivity, no matter how long it takes or how much you invest to achieve it. Resolve today that you are going to practice these principles over and over again until they become second nature.

Practice Self-Discipline in Everything

Discipline yourself to do what you know you need to do to be the very best in your field. Remember the best definition of self-discipline, from Elbert Hubbard: "Self-discipline is the ability to make yourself do what you should do, when you should do it, whether you feel like it or not."

It is easy to do something when you feel like it. It's when you don't feel like it but you force yourself to do it anyway that you move your life and career onto the fast track. What decision do you need to make today in order to start moving toward the top of your field? Whatever the decision is, to get in or to get out, make it today and then get started. This single act can change the whole direction of your life.

Develop Clear Goals and Objectives

Perhaps the most important word in achieving success for the rest of your life is the word *clarity*. Fully 80 percent of your success comes about as the result of your being absolutely clear about what it is you are trying to accomplish. Unfortunately, probably 80 percent or more of failure and frustration comes to people who are vague or fuzzy about what it is they want and how to go about achieving it.

The great oil billionaire H. L. Hunt once said that there are only *two* real requirements for great success. First, he said,

"Decide exactly what it is you want." Most people never do this. Second, he said, "Determine the price you are going to have to pay to get it and then resolve to pay that price!"

You can have just about anything you really want so long as you are willing to pay the price. And nature always demands two things: that you pay the price *in full* and that you pay it *in advance*.

There is a powerful seven-step formula that you can use to set and achieve your goals for the rest of your life. Every successful person uses this formula or some variation of it. As a result, they achieve vastly more than the average person. And so can you. Here it is.

Seven Steps to Goal-Achievement

Step One: Decide exactly what you want in each area of your life. Become a "meaningful specific" rather than a "wandering generality." Decide how much you want to earn. Decide how much you want to weigh. Decide the kind of family, relationships, and lifestyle you want to enjoy. Decide the exact amount you want to accumulate before you retire. The very act of deciding clearly what you want dramatically increases the likelihood that you will achieve it.

Step Two: Write it down, clearly and in detail. Always think on paper. A goal that is not in writing is not a goal at all. It is merely a *wish*. It has no energy behind it. When you take your goals out of your imagination and crystallize them on paper, you actually program them into your subconscious mind, where they take on a power of their own.

Step Three: Set a deadline for your goal. A deadline acts as a forcing system in your subconscious mind. It motivates you to do the things necessary to make your goal come true. If it is a big enough goal, set sub-deadlines as well. Don't leave this to chance.

Step Four: Make a list of everything that you can think of that you are going to have to do to achieve your goal. When you think of new tasks and activities, write them on your list until your list is complete.

Step Five: Organize your list into a plan. Decide what you will have to do first and what you will have to do second. Decide what is more important and what is less important. And then write out your plan on paper, the same way you would develop a blueprint to build your dream house.

A plan is merely a list of activities organized by sequence and priority. It gives you a track to run on. Every minute spent in planning saves ten minutes in executing the plan and achieving the goal. All successful people have written goals and plans.

Step Six: Take action on your plan. Do something. Do anything. But get busy. Get going. Don't delay. As Confucius said, "A journey of a thousand leagues begins with a single step."

Step Seven: This is perhaps the most important of all. Do something every day that moves you in the direction of your most important goal at the moment. Develop the discipline of doing something that moves you forward 365 days a year. You will be absolutely astonished at how much you accomplish when you utilize this formula in your life every single day.

Goal-Setting Exercise

Here is an exercise that can change your life: Take a blank sheet of paper and write out *ten goals* that you want to accomplish in the next twelve months. Write each of these goals in the present tense, as if a year has passed and you have already achieved the goal. Start each of these goals with the word *I*.

For example, you could write down goals such as, "I earn xxx dollars each year." Or, "I weigh xxx pounds." Or, "I drive such-and-such new car." Your subconscious mind only accepts instructions when they are phrased in the *present tense* and when they are preceded with the word *I*.

Select Your Number One Goal

Once you have your list of ten goals, select the most important goal on that list. Ask yourself, "What one goal, if I achieved it right now, would have the greatest positive impact on my life?"

Whatever it is, put a circle around it. Then write it at the top of a new sheet of paper and set a deadline, make a list, organize the list into a plan, take action on your plan, and do something every day until your goal is achieved. This exercise has made more people successful than perhaps any other goal-setting exercise ever developed.

Resolve to become intensely *goal-oriented*. Think and talk about your goals all the time. Write them and rewrite them. Review them every day. Continually look for better ways to achieve them.

Enacting this combination of a goal-setting formula and a goal-setting exercise will have more of a positive impact on your life than almost anything else you could ever do. Do it today.

Plan Every Day in Advance

Daily planning is absolutely essential for doubling your productivity and your income. You should practice the Six P Formula for high achievement. This formula spells out the message, "Proper Prior Planning Prevents Poor Performance."

Proper planning is the mark of the professional. All successful men and women take a good deal of time to plan their activities in advance. Remember the 90/10 Principle, which says that the 10 percent of time that you spend planning your activities before you begin will save you as much as 90 percent of the time necessary to perform those activities once you start work.

Always Think on Paper

Something wonderful happens between your head and your hand when you write out your plans, in detail, on paper, before you begin. Writing actually sharpens your thinking, stimulates your creativity, and enables you to focus far better than if you were just trying to work everything out in your mind.

Begin with a List

Begin by making a *master list* of everything you can think of that you have to do in the long-term. This master list then becomes the central-control list for your life. Whenever you think of something new that you have to do, or want to do, write it down on the master list.

At the beginning of each month, make a *monthly list* covering everything that you can think of that you will have to do in the coming weeks. Then, break your monthly list down into a *weekly list* and specify exactly when you are going to start and complete the tasks that you have decided upon for your month. Finally, and perhaps most importantly, make a *daily list* of your activities, preferably the night before so that your subconscious mind can work on your list while you sleep.

Always work from a list. When something new comes up during the day, write it down on your list before you do it. As you work, you tick off each item as you complete it. This gives you an ongoing sense of accomplishment and a feeling of personal progress. Crossing off items one by one motivates you and actually gives you more energy. A list serves as a scorecard and makes you feel like a winner. It tells you where you are making progress and what you have to do the next day.

According to time-management experts, working from a list will increase your productivity by 25 percent from the very first day. All highly effective people think on paper and work from written lists.

Use the ABCDE Method to Set Priorities

This is one of the most powerful time-management techniques for setting priorities that you will ever learn. And the beauty of this method lies in the fact that it is so simple and easy to use and apply.

The key to doubling your productivity, in any area of your work or at any time of your life, is to select your *most valuable task* and then discipline yourself to work on that task until it is complete. All of time management revolves around helping you clarify, in your own mind, before you start, the most important thing you could possibly be doing.

The way that you determine your highest priority at any moment is to think about the potential *consequences* of doing or not doing a particular task. A task that is important is one that can have major consequences if it is done or not done. All highly productive people think continually about possible consequences as they plan and organize their activities.

With the ABCDE Method, you make a list before you begin work of everything that you have to do. You then go through the list carefully and put one of these letters next to each item on the list.

Important and Unimportant

An "A" item is something that is very important. This is something that you must do, something that has *serious* consequences associated with either doing it or not doing it. Put an A next to every key task on your list.

A "B" item is something that you *should* do, but it is not as important as an A task. There are consequences associated with doing it or not doing it but they are only mild consequences that don't last for long.

A "C" item is something that would be *nice* to do but for which there are no consequences at all. Phoning a friend, going for coffee, reading the newspaper, or chatting with a coworker are all things that are nice to do, but they have absolutely no consequences for your career or your success.

Follow the Rules

The rule is that you should never do a B item when there is an A item left undone. You should never do a C item when there is a B item left undone. You must be very disciplined about this.

A "D" item is an item that you delegate or outsource to someone else who can do it as well or almost as well as you. The rule is that you should delegate everything possible to free up more time for you to concentrate on your A activities.

E stands for *eliminate*. These are items that are of such low priority that you could eliminate them completely and it would make no difference at all. Sometimes the disciplined act of eliminating low-value tasks can simplify your life and free up enough time for you to accomplish those tasks that have the greatest possible consequences for you.

Once you have applied the ABCDE Formula to your list, go back over the list and organize your A tasks by priority. Put an *A-1* next to your most important task, an *A-2* next to your second-most-important task, and so on.

Then, begin immediately on your A-1 task and discipline yourself to stay at it until it is finished. This simple ABCDE Formula alone will double your productivity.

Separate the Urgent from the Important

Everything that you have to do during the day can be separated into one of four categories. These categories are determined by designating tasks as urgent or not urgent and important or not important.

The first type of task is *both urgent and important.* This is something that you have to do immediately. It is a job that is "in your face." Urgent and important tasks, such as telephone calls, meetings, customer calls, and emergencies are almost always determined by *other people.* They are vital requirements of your job. You cannot put them off without causing serious problems. Most people spend all day long doing things that are both urgent and important.

The Quadrant of Effectiveness

The second category of tasks comprises those actions that are *important but not urgent.* These are the items that usually have the greatest possible long-term consequences, items such as personal renewal, upgrading your knowledge and skills, physical fitness and exercise, and spending time with your family.

An item that is important but not urgent is an item that can be put off until later. But tasks and activities that are not urgent but important sooner or later become very urgent indeed—a term paper in college, for instance, or a report for your boss or for one of your clients.

Don't Waste Time

The third category of tasks is made up of those items that are *urgent but not important.* These may be telephone calls, emails, text messages, coworkers dropping in to see you, casual conversations about what was on television, and so on. You may engage in these activities at work, but they have no impact on your success. Many people delude themselves into thinking that they are actually working when they are doing things that are urgent but unimportant. This is a great time waster and a killer of careers and potential.

Wastes of Time

The greatest time wasters of all are those activities that are *neither urgent nor important*. These are completely useless activities, things that you do during the day that are completely irrelevant and have no consequences at all, such as reading the newspaper, calling home to see what's for dinner, or going shopping. They contribute nothing to your company or your personal goals.

The key to doubling your productivity is, first of all, to spend more time doing things that are urgent and important, and, second, to work on activities that are urgent but not important *at the moment*. You also increase your productivity by refusing to do things that are not important at all.

Always ask yourself, "What are the long-term potential consequences of doing this task? What would happen if I did not do it at all?" And whatever your answer is, let it guide you in your choice of priorities.

The Law of Forced Efficiency

This law says that "There is never enough time to do everything, but there is always enough time to do the most important things."

Whenever you are put under significant pressure to complete an important task, a task for which there are significant consequences, you put your head down and get the job done by the dead-line. Many people cannot discipline themselves to get the job done in advance. They say that they work best under pressure. However, no one works best under pressure. This is just a justification for poor time management. When you are under pressure, not only do you experience more stress but you also make more mistakes. These mistakes often necessitate that the job be redone at a later time.

There are four excellent questions that you can ask to increase your efficiency and double your productivity.

Question One: What is the highest-value use of my time?

What is it that you do that contributes the greatest value to your work and to your life? What is it that you do that pays the very most or yields the highest rewards to you and your company? Talk to your boss and to the people around you. Ask for input. You must be absolutely clear about the answer to this question and work on these high-value activities all the time.

Question Two: Why am I on the payroll?

Exactly what have you been hired to do? And of all the things that you have been hired to do, what are the few whose results most determine your success in your job? These are the activities that you need to focus on all day long.

Question Three: What can you and *only* you do that, if done well, can make a real difference?

Every minute of every day, there is only one answer to this question. It is the task that, if you don't do it, doesn't get done. But if you do it and you do it well, it can make a major difference to both your company and yourself. Whatever it is, you should be working on it above all else. This is where you can make your greatest contribution.

Question Four: Perhaps the best time-management question of all is: what is the most valuable use of my time, right now?

Whatever your answer, be sure that *that* is what you are doing at the moment.

Your ability to ask and answer these questions on a regular basis will keep you on track and performing at your best. Disciplining yourself to work only on the tasks uncovered by these questions will double your productivity. *What is the most valuable use of your time, right now?*

Practice Creative Procrastination

Here is an idea for you: practice *creative procrastination* with the 80/20 Rule. Since you can't do everything, you have to procrastinate on *something*. Therefore, discipline yourself to procrastinate on the 80 percent of activities that contribute very little value to your life and your results.

The average person procrastinates on high-value tasks, but this is not for you. You must hold your own feet to the fire and procrastinate deliberately and continuously on those low-value items that have very few consequences if they are done or not.

Before you start work, always check to make sure that what you are doing is in the top 20 percent of all the things you could be doing. Procrastinate on the rest.

Work at Your Energy Peaks

One of the most important requirements for high productivity is a high level of physical, mental, and emotional energy. Most highly productive, highly successful, highly paid people have higher levels of energy, sustained over longer periods of time.

To generate and maintain high levels of energy, you need to practice proper eating, proper exercise, and proper rest. You need to eat light, nutritious, high-protein foods and avoid fats, sugars, white-flour products, pasta, potatoes, candy, soft drinks, and desserts of all kinds.

You need to get regular exercise, three to five days per week, thirty to sixty minutes each day. I have always been amazed to find that marathon and triathlon runners, people who sometimes exercise vigorously several hours a day, are often among the highest-paid and most productive people in their fields. There seems to be a direct relationship between physical fitness and energy on the one hand and high levels of productivity on the other.

Get Lots of Rest

Especially be sure to get lots of rest, particularly if you are working hard. You need at least seven or eight hours of sleep per night and sometimes even more. You need to take at least one full day off each week and two full weeks off each year if you want to perform at your best.

Identify the times of day when you are the brightest and most alert. For some people, this is the morning. For others it is the afternoon or evening. Whatever it is for you, you should schedule your most creative and demanding tasks during the time of day when you are at your very best. Especially you should do creative work, such as writing reports and proposals, at your energy peaks.

Perhaps your most valuable asset in your work is your ability to think well and perform effectively. Maximum performance and productivity require that you take excellent care of your physical and mental health and that you work at your most important jobs when you are experiencing your highest levels of energy. This is a major key to higher output and greater success.

Practice Single-Handling with Key Tasks

Single-handling is one of the most powerful of all time-management techniques. This technique alone will boost your productivity by 50 percent or more the very first day you begin practicing it. When you make single-handling a habit, you can double your productivity even if you do nothing else recommended in this book.

The way it works is simple. Make a list of everything you have to do on a particular day. Then, select the most important item on your list, the highest-value use of your time. Start work on that most important task and discipline yourself to stay at it until it is 100 percent complete.

Andrew Carnegie, who started as a day laborer in a Pittsburgh steel plant and became one of the richest men in the world, attributed much of his wealth and success to this simple rule. He said that it transformed his life and the lives of everyone who ever worked for him.

Remember, the two keys to success are *focus* and *concentration*. Your ability to concentrate single-mindedly, without diversion or distraction, on one thing, the most important thing, and stay with it until it is complete, will contribute more to your success than any other habit you will ever develop.

Huge Time Savings

The fact is that if you start a task and then put it aside, and then come back to it later and start again, you have to review and remind yourself where you left off. This takes several minutes or more, and can eventually increase the amount of time required to perform that task by 500 percent.

On the other hand, if you pick up a task and discipline yourself to stay at it until it is done, you can *decrease* the amount of time it takes to do that task by as much as 80 percent. This is one of the great secrets of time management and high productivity. And it is a habit that you can develop by practice and repetition.

There are two payoffs from single-handling. The first is that you will soon become one of the most productive and *highest-paid* people in your field. The second and even more important payoff is that every time you complete a major task you get an endorphin rush. Your brain releases a chemical that gives you a feeling of well-being. You feel happy all over. Your self-esteem goes up. You feel energized and motivated and eager to start another task. Single-handling is one of the most important of all success principles ever discovered.

Eat That Frog!

There is an old saying that goes like this: "If the very first thing you do each morning is get up and eat a live frog, you can have the satisfaction of knowing that this is probably the worst thing that is going to happen to you all day long."

And there is another observation that says, "If you have to eat a live frog, it doesn't pay to sit and look at it for too long."

Your "frog" is the biggest, ugliest, hardest, most challenging, but most important task that you have to do at any given time or on any given day.

The jobs that can make the greatest difference in your career and in your life are invariably big, hard jobs. These are the very jobs that you are most likely to procrastinate on. These are the jobs that you keep putting off, even though you know how important they are, or can be, if you get them done.

The High-Performance Formula

Here is the formula for single-handling. Make a list the night before of everything that you have to do the next day. Organize the list by priority, using the ABCDE Method. Select your A-1 task, the most important thing you have to do tomorrow, and put it in the center of your desk or workplace before you quit for the day.

Then, first thing in the morning, before you check your email, make any telephone calls, read the newspaper, or talk with your coworkers, discipline yourself to start work on that task and stay with it until it is 100 percent complete. Discipline yourself to "eat your frog" every morning until it becomes a habit.

This starts your day with a *bang*. From that moment on, you will have more energy, become more focused, and work at a higher tempo. You will always get far more done every day that you eat your frog first thing.

Incredible Growth Rates

About five years ago, I was conducting a strategic-planning exercise for a $30-million company. I told them the story about eating their frog first thing in the morning. They liked the story so much that, at the following Christmas, every executive in the company received a brass frog to put on his or her desk, to remind them all of the importance of this principle.

Within five years, the company's annual sales jumped from $30 million per year to over $100 million per year. And throughout the company, the executives that I continue to work with proudly point out the brass frogs on their desks and tell me what a difference the idea has made in their personal productivity. Try it for yourself.

Organize Your Workspace

Highly productive people work from a clean desk and a clean workspace. Inefficient, unproductive, confused people look the part. Their workplaces often look as if a grenade has gone off, scattering papers and files everywhere. This is not for you.

Make it a habit to clean off your workspace and work from a clean desk all the time, even if you have to take everything off your desk and put it behind you on the floor or on a credenza. Keep your desk clean!

Fully 30 percent of working time today is spent looking for something that has been misplaced in some way. When people say that they work better from a messy desk, it turns out not to be true at all. When these same people are forced to clean up their workspace and work on one item at a time, their productivity doubles within twenty-four hours. It amazes them to learn the truth.

Use the TRAF Formula

Use what is called the TRAF Formula on all your papers.

The first letter, *T*, stands for *toss*. Your wastebasket, or your delete button, is among the most helpful time-management tools in your office. Throw away and delete everything that you possibly can, before you get distracted reading through it. This is especially true for direct-mail advertising, unnecessary subscriptions for magazines, spam email, newspapers, and any other material that you have no need of.

The second letter, *R*, stands for *refer*. This is something that someone else should deal with. Make a note on it, and send it off. Forward it to someone else. Take every opportunity to delegate everything you possibly can so that you have more time to do those things that only you can do.

The third letter, *A*, stands for *action*. Use a special file or folder for this purpose. Your Action file contains everything that you have to take action on in the foreseeable future. By putting things in your Action file you deal with them and get them out of the way.

And the final letter, *F*, stands for *file*. These are papers and documents that you will need to have available to you at a later time.

But remember, before you file anything, that 80 percent of all items that are filed or stored are never referred to again. When you make a note to file something, you are often creating work for someone else. Be sure that it is necessary before you file it.

Time to Get Organized

There are time-management specialists today who charge several hundred dollars to help executives clear up their desks and organize their offices. One of the first things these experts do is help their clients go through the piles of material or junk email that the executive has been saving up to read at a later time. Here is the rule: if you have not read it in six months, it's junk. Delete it or throw it away.

My motto for keeping my office clean is "When in doubt, throw it out!" This applies to email, old magazines, old newsletters, books, and anything else that is cluttering up your life.

Many people are pack rats when it comes to magazines, newsletters, newspapers, and other information that comes in the door. This inability to throw things out usually comes from a poor childhood or from a parent who had a poor childhood. The fact is that you will never be able to read all the information you receive on a daily basis. You must discipline yourself to throw it away as quickly as you possibly can. Keep your workspace clean, and keep only one thing in front of you at a time. This will dramatically increase your productivity.

Use Travel Time Productively

The two major forms of travel time are driving and flying. You should turn both of these forms of transition time into highly productive work time.

When you drive, always listen to *educational* audio programs. The average person drives his or her car 500–1,000 hours each year. This is about the same amount of time as one or two full-time university semesters. Experts at the University of Southern California recently concluded that you can get the same educational value as from full-time university attendance by simply listening to educational audio programs as you drive from place to place.

Turn your car into a *university on wheels.* View your car as a learning machine, a mobile classroom. Enroll in Automobile University and attend for the rest of your career.

Many people have become highly educated and have moved to the tops of their fields with audio learning. You should do the same. You should resolve from this day forward that your car will never be moving without something educational playing.

Make Flying Time Productive

When you fly, you should use the time productively as well. Time-management experts have found that every hour of work in an airplane is equal to *three hours* of work in a busy office. The reason for this is that you can work without any interruptions at all on an airplane, if you plan it and organize it in advance.

Look upon every flight as an opportunity to get your work done and increase your productivity. Plan your trip in advance. Prepare a work schedule. Write up an agenda for the things that you are going to accomplish when you are in the air. Then pack carefully to be sure that you have everything you need to make it a valuable flight.

When you fly, get to the airport early—at least sixty minutes before your flight departs. This will enable you to clear security and board your flight completely relaxed, with your mind calm and clear. You will be ready to begin working as soon as you are airborne.

Start Work Immediately

Once the plane takes off and you can lower your tray table, pull out your materials and begin working immediately. Resist the temptation to read the magazine in the pocket in front of you or watch the movie that they play on long flights. Don't drink alcohol of any kind. Instead, drink two glasses of water for every hour that you are in the air. This will keep you alert and refreshed and will dramatically cut down on jet lag.

One final rule for traveling: on the outbound leg of the flight, you should work on serious activities that require energy and concentration. Read books and magazines on the return flight when you are tired and not as sharp as you were earlier in the day.

In any case, make every minute count. Don't be like those people who drive around listening to the radio or who board the plane and either drink the whole way or just sit there looking out the window. Turn your car into a mobile classroom and your airline seat into your flying office. Use them both to get ahead and stay ahead of your work.

Get Better at Your Key Tasks

This is one of the best time-management techniques of all. The better you get at the important things you do, the less time it takes you to do them as well as or better than before. The very act of becoming very, very good at your key tasks can double your productivity. It can dramatically increase the quality and quantity of the work you get done and can have an inordinate impact on your income.

Here's an example I use in my seminars: A person who types with two fingers using the hunt-and-peck method will type about 5–8 words per minute. However, with a little bit of practice, that same person can become a touch typist. Within ninety days, and with thirty minutes of practice each day, the average person can get his or her typing speed up to 50–80 words per minute.

Notice what has happened. In just three months, by getting better in this key area, the person who was typing 5–8 words per minute can now type 50–80 words per minute. This is an increase of *ten times* the output and productivity in the same amount of time.

Work in Real Time

This is an extremely important principle for increasing your productivity: develop a *sense of urgency*. Maintain a fast tempo. Develop a bias for action. Pick up the pace. Do it now!

Today, there is an incredible need for speed. People who do things quickly and well are considered smarter, more valuable, and more competent than people who do things slowly.

Make decisions quickly. Fully 80 percent of decisions can be made the moment they come up. Don't delay or procrastinate on them. Slow decision-making simply plugs up your pipeline and puts a drag on your activities.

Complete all quick jobs as soon as they come up as well. Anything that will take you less than two minutes is usually something that you should do immediately. Always think about how much time it will take you to ramp up and do the job later if you don't do it now.

Take an important phone call immediately and deal with it. Have an important discussion and make a decision to solve the problem right now. Respond to requests from your boss or your customers quickly. Move quickly when need or opportunity arises. Develop a reputation for speed and dependability.

Your goal should be to develop a reputation for being the person who is given the job when it has to be done *fast*. This will open more doors for you than you can imagine. You will attract more and more opportunities if you do more and more things quickly and well.

Doing things quickly, when they come up, is a vital part of doubling your productivity.

Reengineer Your Work

This is one of the most popular and important ways to reduce the time, energy, and expense it takes to get a job done. Most work processes and jobs today are multitask, multistep jobs. There is a series of things that have to be done, from the beginning to the end, to complete the task.

As it happens, many of these jobs have developed over time with inefficiencies built in that no one really thinks about. Many steps are either unnecessary or actually useless. Nonetheless, they remain in the process, expanding the amount of time it takes to do the job.

But this is not for you. Take any large task that you have to do and write down every single step necessary to complete that job, from the initial idea to the finished task. Make a list of the process as if you were giving a blueprint to someone else to do it.

Once you have a list of every single step, set a goal to reduce the number of steps by 30 percent the first time you go through the list. This is almost always possible when you use your creativity.

Look for ways to consolidate several steps into a single step. Look for ways to consolidate several jobs so that they are done by a single person all at the same time. Look for ways to cut back, discontinue, or eliminate steps that are no longer necessary. Always ask, "Why are we doing it this way?" and, "Could there be a *better* way?"

Your ability to *simplify* and *streamline* your life and work so that you get more done in a shorter period of time is a major key to doubling your productivity.

Practice Zero-Based Thinking Continually

As I mentioned before, this is one of the best tools you will ever use to clarify your thinking and improve the quality of your life. Ask yourself on a regular basis, "Is there anything in my life that, if I had it to do over knowing what I now know, I wouldn't get into again today?"

Is there anything you are doing today, any relationship you are in, any investment, that you wouldn't get into if you had it to do over? This is one of the most important questions you ever ask and answer.

When you think of the biggest time wasters, you usually think of unexpected interruptions or telephone calls. However, the biggest time waster of all is for you to continue to pursue a course of action, a job, a career, or a relationship, that is the wrong one for you. Many people waste many years of their lives working at something that they don't particularly like or enjoy, and then in their thirties or forties they have to start all over again in a completely new job in a brand new career.

Keep Asking the Question

Because we are living in a time of rapid change, fully 70 percent of your decisions will turn out to be *wrong* in the fullness of time. This means that everyone is involved in at least one thing that, knowing what they now know, they wouldn't get into again. And the key indicator of a zero-based thinking situation is stress. Whenever you feel chronic stress, dissatisfaction, or unhappiness with any person or situation, you should ask yourself, "Knowing what I now know, would I get into this situation again?"

If your answer is, "No!" then the next question is, How do I get out of this situation, and how quickly should I do it?

Is there any relationship in your life, business, social, or personal, that you wouldn't get into again? Is there any part of your business, any product, service, expenditure, or process that you wouldn't start up again today if you had it to do over?

Is there any investment that you are engaged in today, of time, money, or emotion, that's dragging you down and holding you back and that, knowing what you now know, you wouldn't get into again?

Remember, whatever the situation, it is probably not going to change. In fact, it is probably going to get worse over time. The only question then is this: do you have the courage and character to deal honestly with your life as it really is today?

When you apply zero-based thinking to every part of your life, you will be absolutely amazed at how much better your decisions become, and how much more productive you become at the same time.

Set Clear Posteriorities

You have heard of setting priorities. Priorities are tasks that you do more of and sooner. A *posteriority*, on the other hand, is something that you do *less of* and *later*, if at all.

The fact is that you are already overwhelmed with too much to do and too little time. For you to do something new or different, you must *discontinue* something that you are already doing. You must begin systematically setting posteriorities on activities in your life that are no longer as important as other activities.

Practice what Peter Drucker calls "creative abandonment" with tasks and activities that are no longer as valuable as they were when you first started doing them.

You have too much to do already. Therefore, before you start something new you have to stop doing something old. Picking up a new task requires putting down an old task. Getting in means getting out. Starting up means stopping off.

Look for More Time

Look at your life and your work. What sort of things should you stop doing so that you can free up enough time to do more of the things you should be doing, more of the time?

You can only get your life under control to the degree to which you discontinue lower-value activities. You can only double your productivity when you free up more time to do the things that can have a significant payoff for you in the future.

When I get overloaded with work, I have a little motto that I repeat to myself all the time: All you can do is all you can do.

Whenever you feel overloaded for any reason, whenever you feel that you have too much to do and too little time, stop, take a deep breath, and say to yourself, "All I can do is all I can do."

Then sit down, make a list of everything you have to do, and begin setting posteriorities on your time. Sometimes the word *no* can be the best time-saver of all.

Keep Your Life in Balance ←

The reason you are working is so that you can earn enough to enjoy your family, your health, and the important parts of your personal life. You want to have happy, healthy, harmonious relationships with your spouse and children. You want to be healthy and fit. You want to grow, mentally and spiritually. You want to be as successful as possible in your work and your career so that you have the resources to do all the things that you really care about that have nothing to do with your work.

Unfortunately, most people get the cart before the horse. They become so preoccupied with their work that they lose sight of the reason for wanting to be successful at their work in the first place. This is definitely not for you.

Remember that in life, *relationships are everything*. Fully 85 percent of your success and happiness in life will come from your relationships with other people. Only 15 percent of your happiness will come from your achievements in your work. You must keep your life in balance.

Simplify and Streamline

In my executive coaching, I work with CEOs and high achievers to show them how they can dramatically simplify their lives, reduce their work hours, spend more time with their families, and increase their incomes, all at the same time. Most people doubt that all this is possible until they begin using these techniques.

One executive in our program was working sixty and seventy hours a week and earning about $55,000 a year. After he began simplifying and balancing his life, over a period of five years his income increased to over $300,000 per year while his workweek dropped to thirty-eight hours. You can do very much the same in your life.

The Keys to Balance

The keys to balance are simple. Set your peace of mind, your happiness, and your well-tended home life as your highest goals and organize the rest of your life around them.

Create *blocks of time* to spend with your family. Create time in the evenings, time on the weekends, and time away on vacations. Remember the formula for balance, which is this: it is *quantity* of time at home that counts and *quality* of time at work. And don't mix them up. The simplest of all rules for balance is, Put people first. And of all the people that you put first, put the most important people in your life ahead of everything and everyone else.

When you work, *work all the time you work.* Don't waste time with idle chatting and useless activities. Work all the time. Remember that every minute you waste at work in idle socializing is a minute that you are taking away from your family and your important relationships.

When you get your life in balance, you will actually accomplish more, be paid more, produce more, and have vastly more time with your family. This is the whole reason for wanting to become more productive in the first place.

Be Intensely Action-Oriented

Today, everyone is in a hurry. Your customers did not even know they wanted your product or service before now, and now they want it *yesterday.* People are incredibly impatient. No one will wait in line anymore. The average Web surfer will switch windows in seven or eight seconds if the Internet site does not load fast enough.

The most outwardly identifiable quality of the top performer in every field is that he or she is in constant motion. The top performer takes initiative to get the job done. The top performer takes action over and over again, continually heading toward the goal.

On the other hand, the greatest single obstacle to high performance is the tendency to talk a subject to death. Many people think that talking well and planning continually is the same as execution. But only action is action. Only execution is execution. Only your ability to get the job done really matters.

In the final analysis, you only get paid for *results*. Results are everything. Intense results-orientation goes hand in hand with high productivity and high performance in every area.

Make a decision today that you are going to move quickly when opportunity or need presents itself. Pick up the pace. Take action of some kind. Get on with it!

The good news is that the faster you move, the better you feel. The faster you move, the more you get done. The faster you move, the more energy you have. The faster you move, the more you learn and the more experience you get. And the faster you move, the more you get paid and the faster you get promoted.

Make Every Minute Count

As I said before, we are living in one of the most challenging times in all of human history. But there are few limits to what you can accomplish beyond the limits that you place on yourself. Your job is to become one of the most productive people in your field. Your goal is to develop a reputation for being the person they come to *first* when anyone wants or needs something done.

Your goal is to get paid more and promoted faster. Your goal is to have a wonderful life, and you achieve it by managing your time and doubling your productivity.

Action Exercises:

1. Decide *exactly* what you want, in terms of goals and objectives.

2. Make a list of everything that you have to do today to move you toward the achievement of your goals and objectives.
3. Organize your list by priority using the 80/20 Rule or the ABCDE Method.
4. Select your A-1, your most important single task.
5. First thing each morning, start work *immediately* on your number one task.
6. Discipline yourself to work single-mindedly on your most important task until it is 100 percent complete.
7. Become intensely action-oriented. Keep repeating over and over to yourself the wonderful words "Do it now! Do it now! Do it now!"

CHAPTER EIGHT

Practical Project Management

People do not decide to become extraordinary. They
decide to accomplish extraordinary things.

—SIR EDMUND HILLARY

Some skills are peripheral to success. They are helpful to your career, but they don't determine your level of success or failure. There are other skills, however, that are absolutely essential to your fulfilling your potential, and you must develop them to a fairly high degree if you are to achieve all of your financial and career goals.

One of these absolutely essential skills is the ability to manage projects of various sizes. A project can be defined as *a multitask job*, the kind that you engage in every day in the course of making a living and carrying on the business of your life. To be a success, you must be good at project management.

Avoid the Intelligence Trap

One of the great dangers in project management is feeling that you already know all you need to know about the subject. Too many people take their ability to do several jobs at once, or in a row, for granted. They fall into the *intelligence trap* of the low-performer. They use their intelligence to point out to themselves and to others how confident and capable they already are. They join the ranks of the *unconscious incompetents*. The unconscious incompetent is the person who does not know, and does not know that he or she does not know.

A Basic Life Skill

Project management is an essential skill, and not just for those who build hydroelectric dams or construct huge skyscrapers. You organize and engage in a project each time you go shopping at the grocery store. If you are in sales, every prospect you are working on developing into a regular customer is a project. If you are going out for the evening with another person, you are planning and organizing a project.

Here is a key point: your ability to organize and complete a project successfully is a vital skill for success. It is the essential art of management. It is the way that you *multiply* your abilities and your results. Your ability to manage projects of all kinds is absolutely indispensable to your increasing your value and earning what you are really worth. This skill is the key to achieving financial independence and moving to the top in your field.

Be the Best in Your Field

Many people can type, but few people can type eighty or ninety words a minute without mistakes. Millions of people know how to operate computers, but only a few can use the computer skillfully enough to maximize its capacities in helping them do their work and accomplish their objectives. Many people can sell, but the top 10 percent of salespeople still open 80 percent of the new accounts and make most of the money.

Project management is similar. Everyone knows how to carry out a multitask job. But few people are good at it. Most are partially organized and partially disorganized. They take too much time, spend too much money, and make too many mistakes in getting from Point A to Point B. They don't manage the projects in their lives skillfully because they don't know how critical this ability is to accomplishing virtually everything else they could possibly want in life.

To succeed in life, you need *leverage*. You need the assistance of others. If you want to achieve big things, and live a great life, you need the help of lots of people. You need to be very good at coordinating the activities of several people in a single direction toward a predetermined objective. If you don't develop your skills at project management, you will still be involved in projects, but you will always be a team member and never a team leader.

Outsourcing and Project Management

The economic strength of America is due to many things, and one of the most important is specialization of tasks, or division of labor. This simply means that most people, instead of trying to be jacks-of-all-trades, specialize and become very good at doing one or two things. They delegate everything else.

Today, one of the most popular words in American business is *outsourcing*. This means that instead of hiring or building a capability in-house, you delegate an entire function of your company to another company that specializes in doing only that one task.

Many companies are finding that it is cheaper than doing it themselves to have functions such as payroll, accounting, drop-shipping, manufacturing, assembly, delivery, and distribution, plus a thousand other tasks, done by other companies.

You Are Outsourcing Continually

Your whole life is a process of *outsourcing*. Whether you are aware of it or not, you are continually outsourcing tasks and activities to a hundred other enterprises, such as grocery stores, restaurants, dry cleaners, quick-oil-change franchises, and tailors. You don't bother to learn how to do those things yourself. It is much faster and cheaper for you to turn the tasks over to people who specialize in them. They can do the tasks faster, better, and with fewer mistakes than you ever could. By outsourcing, you free up your time to do more and more of the things that you do best and for which you are paid the most. It is one of the keys to developing the leverage that turns you into a multiplication sign with your talents and abilities.

The Key to High Productivity

In project management, you engage in a systematic and well-organized process of outsourcing the various tasks that need to be done to achieve a particular objective. You develop *synergy* by pulling together the talents and abilities of a lot of people toward the accomplishment of a single goal. By working together as a team, a group of people with different talents can accomplish extraordinary things. And your ability to get all members of a team pulling in the same direction is the key to your maximizing yourself in your life and career.

To unleash the cooperative capabilities of a team of people toward the achievement of a multitask job, the operative word should be *harmony*. One of the most important things you can do is to strive for harmony among the people working with you and for you.

Project Management

Project management is an art. It requires thought and foresight. Whenever you have a large job to do, your very first step is to sit down with a pad of paper and begin to think on paper. As we know, all highly successful men and women think on paper. They write things down before they begin. They make lists, and they make sub-lists. They calculate the numbers. They analyze every detail of a large project beforehand. They think it through from beginning to end. And in so doing they save enormous amounts of time and money, and they often get more done in a few months than the average person gets done in years.

Practice and Discipline

Project management takes practice, as does anything else. It requires self-discipline. It requires the willpower to hold yourself back from plunging into a task before thinking it through. Many people work in a *reactive-responsive* mode. They react to whatever is happening around them, and they respond to however they feel at the moment. They leap into things, and then they leap out. They rush to make judgments and come to decisions, and they take actions without bothering to analyze the situation thoroughly. They make enormous numbers of mistakes and are seen by others as incompetent and disorganized. Don't be one of those people.

When you decide to become excellent at project management, you begin to apply a systematic process such as the one I will describe. Your ability to achieve multitask jobs will give you the ability to control everything else you accomplish. And it's not that difficult to learn.

Start with the Finished Project

In executing any project, the first thing to do is start at the goal and work back. Stephen Covey says, "Begin with the end in mind." Dr. Roberto Assagioli suggests that you begin all activities by creating the ideal result or outcome, either on paper or in your mind, before you proceed to planning and organizing.

Robert Fritz, in his book *The Path of Least Resistance*, says that the most powerful of all organizing principles is a vision of a clear goal to which you, and others, are committed. In his research on peak performers, Dr. Charles Garfield found that a person's ability to project his or her mind forward to the desired end state, to the goal as if it were already achieved, to the task as if it were completed perfectly in every respect, is the starting point of maximum achievement.

Each project begins with your clearly defining exactly what you want to accomplish and what it will look like if it is accomplished perfectly.

Organize Each of the Steps

Once you are clear about your goal, the next step in project management is to organize your list of all the things that will need to be done to get to your goal, the completion of your project. There are two ways to organize a list in project management. The first way is *sequential*. This is where one step follows another. The first task must be completed before the second can be started, the second must be completed before the third can be started, and so on. These are often called *dependent* activities. One activity depends on the successful completion of the previous. This is a key point to remember in managing a project of any size.

The second way to list activities in project management is as *parallel* or *concurrent* activities. These are tasks that can be worked on at the same time, each separate from the others. For example, if you are planning a new brochure or newsletter you could be writing the copy at the same time that you are selecting paper stock or gathering possible photographs to illustrate the content.

Remember the Six P Rule? *Proper Prior Planning Prevents Poor Performance.* Your ability to plan your projects carefully and thoroughly in advance can dramatically increase your productivity.

Once you have the goal in mind, and have listed everything that you must do to achieve the goal, and have organized everything in terms of whether it is sequential or concurrent, you are ready for the core exercise of effective project management. It is the key to your future in the world of work. It is the process of *selection and delegation.*

Selection and Delegation

The bigger the project, the more people will be required to carry it through to successful completion. Your ability to select the right people and then to delegate effectively to them will determine, as much as any other factor, your project's success or failure. A mistake in selection or a miscommunication in delegation can be enough to set it back, have it run over budget, or even derail it completely.

Many men and women have been able to shoot ahead in their careers by taking on a project and then performing in an exemplary fashion. Others have found themselves bypassed for promotion because when they were given a project to carry out, they did not take it seriously enough, and their lack of results undermined their superiors' confidence in their abilities. Project management is serious stuff.

Project Management Problems

Almost all problems in business are management problems, which are in effect project-management problems. This is often why when a new manager comes in he or she replaces everyone on the team. The new manager recognizes that the reason why the job isn't getting done is probably that the person in charge of the multitask job—manufacturing, sales, distribution, or whatever—is not up to the task.

When you build your team, you make a statement about your capability as a manager. As much as 95 percent of your success in the business world will be determined by your ability to select the right people to help you. Most of your problems in business come from attempting to get the job done with difficult or incompetent people.

Your job is to select the very best people available who can do the job. Examine each person's track record carefully. Check references. Talk to other people about the task, and get opinions concerning each individual's ability to do it in an excellent fashion.

Be careful about your choices, and be adamant about assigning key tasks to the very best people. This will save you enormous amounts of time and trouble.

One key point: if you find that you have selected the wrong person, someone who cannot or will not do the job on time to the required level of quality, move quickly to remove and replace the poor performer. One weak person on a team can sabotage the efforts of everyone and demoralize your best people. This replacement of a person who is not working out is a chief responsibility of leadership.

Multiply Yourself with Delegation

Once you have selected the individuals to carry out the specific parts of the project, you must delegate effectively to each of them. Assign specific responsibilities for each task necessary to complete the project to specific individuals. Set deadlines on each task and each part of each task. Explain to each person what is to be done, when it is to be done, what standards of measurement you will use to determine successful performance, and what the overall project will look like when it is complete. Leave nothing to chance. The more people know about the *what* and *why* of the total job, the more capable they will be of carrying out their individual functions.

Lack of clarity is the single greatest contributor to failure in project management. For this reason, it is important that you meet regularly with the members of your team, either individually or together. You keep in touch with them on a regular basis. You keep them informed. You give and receive feedback. And the more important the project is, the more you stay on top of it.

Make the Project Visual

Just as it is important for you to think on paper when organizing a project for yourself, it is helpful for you to use a whiteboard or a flip chart when you are meeting with the members of your team. The more *visual* you can make the project, and the process of achieving the goal, the more likely it is that each task will be completed on schedule and to the standards you have set.

You supervise the project by measuring people's progress toward their individual deadlines. Your supervision of the project is what makes it all come together. The rule is "Inspect what you expect." Never assume anything. Remember, Murphy's laws were developed by men and women managing projects of various sizes.

Murphy's Laws

You know some of these laws:

1. Anything that can go wrong, will go wrong.
2. However much you budget, it will cost more than you expect.
3. However long you allow, it will take longer than you thought.
4. Of all the things that can go wrong, the worst possible thing will go wrong at the worst possible time, and cost the greatest amount of money.

And, of course, there is the corollary to Murphy's laws: *Murphy was an optimist.*

Identify the Limiting Step

In project management, there is always a critical event, or *limiting step*. This is the one factor that determines the speed at which you complete the project. This is the one task that absolutely, positively has to be done to a set standard for the project to be successful. It is in this area that you must take personal responsibility and focus your attention on making sure that everything is done right. Keep your eyes on the ball, even if you delegate or outsource part or all of the task.

You can use project management to develop a new account, to increase your income, to attain a high level of physical health and fitness, to take a vacation, to move across the country, to start and build a business, to write a book, to paint a picture, or to sail a catamaran around the world.

Gain the Winning Edge

Throughout your career, the proper use of project-management techniques such as those we have discussed here can give you the winning edge. It can enable you to kick on the afterburners for your life and your career. The skill of project management will enable you to move ahead further and faster than you ever could without it. Although the steps to project management are simple, the skill of project management is complex, and it is vital to your success.

The cumulative results of your developing the skills of project management will enable you to accomplish bigger and better tasks with greater responsibilities and higher income—with greater rewards of all kinds. Project management is an essential skill for you in earning what you are really worth, and you can learn it with practice.

Action Exercises:

1. Select one project that you are working on right now or that you would like to complete, and follow the professional approach suggested in this chapter.

2. Determine the ideal result or outcome that would occur if the project were completed perfectly. Write it down.

3. Make a list of every step that you will have to take to complete the project on time and on budget.

4. Organize the list of activities by sequence and priority, those tasks that must be done in order and those tasks that can be done at any time.

5. Decide exactly who is going to be responsible for the completion of each task or function within each task, and decide the schedule for completion.

6. Select the members of your team and discuss the project with them in detail so that each person knows exactly what he or she is expected to do.

7. Take action immediately, and then continuously monitor and supervise the activities of the team until the project is completed satisfactorily.

CHAPTER NINE

Put People First

Pretend that every person you meet has a sign around his or her neck that says, "Make me feel important." Not only will you succeed in sales, you will succeed in life.

—MARY KAY ASH

Your ability to get along well with others will have a greater impact on your earning ability than any other quality. To earn what you're really worth, you have to become an expert in working with others.

In his book *Frames of Mind*, Dr. Howard Gardner of Harvard University made the revolutionary claim that individuals possess several forms of intelligence. He concluded that we are all intelligent in a variety of ways, and that even if we didn't receive great grades in school, we can still be extremely intelligent in other areas. Two of these areas are included in *intrapersonal intelligence* and *interpersonal intelligence.*

*Intra*personal intelligence is defined as how well you get along with yourself. It is how well you know yourself and understand yourself, and how clear you are about your strengths and weaknesses, your values, opinions, goals, and dreams. People with high levels of this kind of intelligence are extremely aware of who they are and who they are not. This enables them to be honest and objective with themselves, to recognize their strengths and weaknesses, and, as a result, to be more honest and objective with others.

Intrapersonal intelligence is the foundation upon which the second kind of intelligence, *inter*personal intelligence, is built. Interpersonal intelligence is an ability to *communicate*, *negotiate*, and *interact with*, and *persuade* and *influence* other people. People who are successful in businesses requiring active interaction with other people, such as salespeople, managers, counselors, consultants, and lawyers, all have a high degree of interpersonal intelligence.

Increase Your Intelligence

You can increase your intelligence in any area by *learning* and *practicing* in that area. And perhaps the most important intelligence you can consciously and purposefully develop is your interpersonal intelligence. That's because forming and maintaining relationships is vital to both your professional success and your self-concept.

Our personalities are largely shaped by the way people react to us. Our only indication as to who we are when we are young is the way people treat us. If people treat us with kindness, respect, and good humor, we eventually conclude that we are pretty good people who deserve kindness, respect, and proper treatment. These attitudes continue into adult life.

Three Deep Needs

Psychologists have identified three basic social needs that we all have: *inclusion*, *control*, and *affection*. The first, inclusion, is the need to feel that we belong, that we are included in families, work groups, social groups, business organizations, and professional associations. We need to feel wanted, accepted, and important.

The second social need we have is for control. Psychologists have concluded that the basis of a positive mental attitude is a sense of control. We are happy to the degree to which we feel we have control over our lives. We are unhappy to the degree to which we feel out of control, or controlled by someone or something else. Most stress is caused by feeling out of control of some part of our life that is important to us.

The third social need we all have is for affection. It is hard to live without the knowledge that someone cares about us. Sometimes just knowing that even one single person somewhere cares about us is enough to give meaning to our entire lives.

You Are a Work in Progress

In publishing circles there is an expression—*a work in progress.* This is a book that has been scheduled for publication but is not yet complete; the author is still working on it, at one stage or another.

Each of us is a work in progress. Each of us is born and grows up inexperienced in the ways of the world. Over time, and with a lot of hard knocks, we develop a greater depth of character and personality. And all of our lessons are learned in the crucible of human contact.

There are certain parts of your personality that will remain completely untouched and undeveloped unless and until you enter into deep, meaningful, intimate, emotional relationships with people you love and who love you in return. It is only then that you develop the depth of personality that makes you a more fully mature, fully functioning, and fully integrated individual.

The Perfection of Character

On the wall of my first karate dojo was a sign that said, "The ultimate aim of karate lies not in victory or defeat, but in the perfection of the character of its participants."

I think that is the ultimate aim of life as well—the perfection of the character of its participants. And it is hardly possible for you to become everything you are capable of becoming without the lessons that come through relationships with people for whom you care deeply, and who, in turn, care deeply for you.

Seven Essential Principles

Relationships can be extremely complicated, but to build and maintain quality relationships requires only a few basic principles. Let me give you seven:

Principle One: The first is the principle of *trust.* All relationships are ultimately based on trust. To build trust, you always keep your word. You remain consistent and dependable in everything you say and do. You become the kind of person who is utterly reliable in every situation. You never do or say anything that can shake this foundation of trust upon which your relationships are built.

Principle Two: The second principle is *respect.* Taking time to deliberately express your respect for the uniqueness of an individual makes him or her feel valuable and important. By demonstrating that kind of respect, you build and enhance the quality of your relationships.

Principle Three: The third principle for success in relationships is *communication.* In communicating well with another person, time is the critical factor. The value of a relationship can increase for both you and the other person depending on *the amount of time that you invest.* When you take the time to focus on the important issues of a relationship, you open the channels of communication. And when you listen calmly, quietly, and with total attention, you demonstrate the respect you have for the other person, and you deepen the level of trust between you.

Principle Four: The fourth principle is *courtesy.* When you say please and thank you on a regular basis to the people in your life, you make them feel better about themselves and about what they are doing. You raise their self-esteem. Alas, it is often with the people we care about most that we are the least courteous and polite. Emmet Fox once wrote, "If you must be rude, be rude to strangers. But save your company manners for your family."

Principle Five: *Caring.* The greatest gift that you can give to others is the gift of unconditional love and acceptance. The kindest thing you can do is refrain from criticizing, condemning, or complaining to them or concerning them.

Think of yourself as a people-*builder* rather than a people-*basher.* Catch others doing something right. Always look for ways to make people feel more valuable, more respected, and more loved.

The three most powerful words in any relationship are the words *I love you.* Repeat them as often as possible and in as many different ways as possible to the most important people in your life.

Principle Six: The sixth principle for success with people is a combination of *praise* and *appreciation* for everything that others do for you, both large and small. When you say thank you to another person for something they do for you, they feel better about themselves, and they want to do more. When you praise someone for something they have accomplished, their self-esteem goes up. They feel valuable and important. And there is a boomerang effect that causes your own self-esteem to go up, exactly as if you yourself had been praised or appreciated.

Principle Seven: The seventh principle for success in relationships is simply *helpfulness*, especially with those people with whom you live. Your constant willingness to step in and do little things to alleviate the burdens felt by your spouse and children is always appreciated and respected. This willingness to share, to contribute, to help each other is an important facet of lasting relationships.

Perhaps the most important thing you ever do in life is build and maintain long-term, happy, healthy, fulfilling relationships with people you love and who love you. When you make everything else secondary to this central purpose, you will find yourself enjoying happiness and rewards in exponential proportion to the efforts you put in.

Action Exercises:

1. To get along well with others, practice unconditional acceptance by smiling each time you meet a boss or coworker.
2. Express appreciation regularly by saying thank you for anything and everything that people do that is positive or helpful.
3. Admire and compliment people for their clothes, cars, accessories, personality traits, and accomplishments.
4. Express approval, and praise people for large and small achievements, thereby satisfying for them one of the deepest cravings of human nature, to feel valuable and important.
5. Be agreeable, even if you don't agree. Look for something good in what the other person has said and acknowledge that.
6. Refuse to criticize or condemn people for any reason, either to their faces or behind their backs.
7. Continually see ways to increase people's self-esteem and self-respect so that they feel good about themselves, and about you.

CHAPTER TEN

Powerful Problem Solving and Decision-Making

Thought is the original source of all wealth, all success, all material gain, all great discoveries and inventions, and all achievement.

—CLAUDE M. BRISTOL

To earn what you are worth, you must continually increase your value to others and to your work. One of the most important skills or qualities of leaders and effective people in every area is the ability to solve problems and make good decisions that lead to more and better results.

All of life is a series of problems to be solved and difficulties to be overcome. Your ability to solve the problems you meet at your level is essential to your being paid more and promoted faster. Success is the ability to solve problems. Leadership is the ability to solve problems. And the real reward for solving problems is that you get even bigger problems to solve.

Fortunately, effective problem solving and decision-making are learnable skills that you can develop with practice and by learning to tap into the incredible powers of your mind.

Focus on Solutions

Your life and work will be a continuous succession of problems. You will have problem after problem, all day long and into the evenings. In fact, where there are no problems, the work can be automated and done by a machine. And the more minor problems that are automated, the more important and valuable you become in solving problems of greater complexity.

The only interruption in this continuous flow of problems will be the occasional *crisis*. If you are living a normal life, you will have a crisis every two or three months. Your ability to deal effectively with the inevitable and unavoidable crises is a key measure of your character and your competence.

Focus on the Future

Solution-oriented people are the most valuable people in any organization. You can change your mind-set from negative to positive in a single moment by switching your thoughts from the problem to the solution. Instead of asking or worrying about who did what and who is to blame, you should ask, What do we do now?

The more you focus on finding solutions, the more solutions you find. The better you get at solving problems, the bigger the problems you will be given to solve, and the more money, power, and position you will be given to go along with the size of the problems. In fact, your entire life and career will be determined by your ability to solve the problems that you meet at your level. When you do solve them, you automatically get moved to a higher level, exactly as you get moved to a higher grade in school when you have passed the exams in the previous grade.

Solve Problems Systematically

Here is a seven-step method that you can use for the rest of your career to deal effectively with any problem that comes along.

Step 1: Define the problem clearly. What exactly is the problem? Get the facts. Get the real facts. Not the apparent facts or the obvious facts, but the real facts of the situation. It is amazing how much time and energy is wasted attempting to solve problems when the people involved are not even clear what the problem is in the first place.

Step 2: Ask what all the possible causes of this problem are. How and why did it happen? Sometimes, this exercise alone will suggest a solution.

Step 3: Ask what all the possible solutions are. The more possible solutions you can come up with, the more likely it is that you will come up with the ideal solution.

Step 4: Make a decision. Any decision is usually better than no decision at all.

Step 5: Assign responsibility for carrying out the decision. *Who* exactly is going to do what, and when, and to what standard?

Step 6: Set a schedule of reporting and a *standard* to measure whether or not the decision has been successful. A solution without a standard or a deadline is really not a solution at all.

Step 7: Task yourself or someone else with taking definite action to implement the solution and resolve the problem.

Become solution-oriented in your approach toward life and work. Be the kind of person people bring their problems to because you always have a good idea to solve them. The more you focus on solutions, the smarter you become and the better solutions you come up with. The people who are the best at problem solving are the highest-paid and fastest promoted in any organization.

The Most Powerful Computer

Just imagine that someone gave you a simple but powerful computer that had the capacity to answer any question or solve any problem you would ever face. All you would have to do is program the problem into the computer properly. Then, at exactly the right time, it would bring you exactly the answer that you needed. The answer would always be perfectly correct for you.

The fact is that you already have such a computer, and it's installed right between your ears. The only real difference between extremely effective people and those who are not happy with their results is the degree to which they use this amazing computer. The wonderful discovery is that you can easily learn to use it on a regular basis. When you do, you will immediately start to benefit by making better decisions and getting better results.

To understand how this marvelous computer works, let's begin by studying your brain. Your brain is divided into two hemispheres, commonly called the *right brain* and the *left brain*. Extensive research suggests that each part of the brain is responsible for specific functions.

Two Brains in One

Your left brain tends to be responsible for linear, sequential, orderly, and mathematical functions. It is practical, analytical, and skeptical. It is the part of the brain that deals with categories and concrete things. Your left brain deals with the verbal, the numerical, and the scientific. It is the *engineering* half of the brain, and it is primarily focused on processing facts in a step-by-step fashion.

Your right brain, on the other hand, is very different. It is holistic and spontaneous. While your left brain deals with individual details, your right brain deals with complete pictures and fully integrated ideas and situations. Your right brain is also in charge of your creative, musical, and artistic abilities. It is responsible for dancing, and singing, and laughter. Your right brain is responsible for the intuitive processes of thinking, feeling, problem solving, and decision-making.

Unlock Your Full Potential

When you learn to harmonize the operations of both of these brains so they work in cooperation, you begin to perform at exceptional levels. Men and women begin to unlock their full potentials when they utilize the marvelous capacities of the right brain, especially for making important decisions.

An *intuitive* decision, one that comes to you from within, is always superior to anything that you can arrive at by simply considering the facts and details. An intuitive decision integrates all of your knowledge about a subject simultaneously and gives you an answer that is a synthesis superior to anything you could have worked out in a step-by-step fashion. This is why the men and women who are at the top of virtually all organizations tend to be extremely intuitive in the way they solve problems and make decisions for themselves and others.

Intuition is often referred to as the still, small voice within. This inner voice is like an unfailing guide or mechanism that always tells you the correct thing to do or say. The more you trust it and believe in it, the better and more accurately it works for you. Your ability to use your intuitive decision-making powers precedes and predicts your success and effectiveness in virtually everything you do.

Four Mental Qualities

To trigger your intuition and tap into higher levels of your mind on a regular basis, you need to have four particular mental qualities. The first is a complete *trust* and *belief*, almost a childlike faith, in your intuition, and a willingness to just "go with the flow" of your inner mind. Your intuition functions effortlessly and works best when you stop *trying* to make something happen and instead just let go and accept whatever solution comes to you.

The second mental quality that enables you to use your intuition more efficiently is a *positive mental attitude*. By this, I mean that you remain calm, relaxed, and cheerful about outcomes. A positive mental attitude has been described as a "constructive response to stress and adversity." When you respond in a relaxed, easygoing way, you create the mental climate that enables your brain to function at its best, and this is what triggers your intuition.

Expect the Best

The third mental quality for enhancing your intuition is an attitude of *confident expectation*. The more positive and confident you are, the sharper and quicker your intuitions and solutions will be. Make it a practice to confidently expect things to go well for you.

Look for the valuable lesson in every difficulty and adversity. Seek out the advantage or benefit in each setback or obstacle that you face. Your conscious decision to keep your mind focused on the good parts of your situation, coupled with your refusal to dwell on the negative parts, will enable your mind to function at its best to help you achieve your goals.

The fourth mental quality for intuitive decision-making is *listening*. Women tend to be better at listening to their intuition than men are. This is probably why women's intuition is so much more respected than men's. However, men and women have the same intuitive abilities. All they have to do is listen to what these abilities are telling them on a regular basis. Most of our mistakes in life result from ignoring our intuition or refusing to listen to it because we think that by doing so we will be better off. This always turns out to be a mistake.

Three Places to Use Your Intuition

There are three areas where you can use your intuition continually to make better decisions and avoid costly mistakes.

1. Personal relationships: Whether the relationship in question is with your spouse or child or a friend, your intuition will always tell you the right thing to do or say. All you need to do in any situation is quietly turn to your intuition and *listen*, and then say or do what seems most proper and natural.

    In my experience, one of the major reasons for problems in relationships is that one or both parties are ignoring their intuition and refusing to listen to it or act on it. People get into or out of relationships or make decisions in their interactions with others even when, deep inside, they know that they are doing the wrong thing. If ever you go against your intuition, your "gut feeling," you almost always create a problem that is bigger and more difficult to deal with than if you had listened to your intuition in the first place.

2. Professional relationships: If you listen quietly to your inner voice, you will always get a good feeling about the right thing to do, or not do, in every business situation.

    If you are in sales, whenever you are with a prospect or a client you can rely completely on your intuition to tell you what to do and what to say, and when you follow it, you will always find that it is leading you toward the right things. Many salespeople have told me of their having a sudden impulse to bring up a particular subject in a sales interview and later finding that it was exactly the right thing to say at exactly the right time. All top salespeople tend to trust their intuition and listen to it continually in their sales work.

3. Making choices: Whether you are communicating or negotiating or buying or selling, or accepting or leaving a job, you are always making choices of one kind or another. Some of these choices are not important, but many of them have potentially serious long-term consequences.

   Accepting a job, negotiating a salary, or going to work for a particular company at a particular time can have a significant impact on the whole direction of your life. Investing, or spending, or borrowing money for any reason can have significant long-term consequences. Any decision that has results that last long after you have made the decision is the kind of decision to which you need to apply your amazing intuitive powers.

Increase Your Powers

Fortunately, there are some specific steps that you can take to increase the powers of your intuitive mind. You can begin by selecting any problem or situation you are dealing with at the current time and programming it into your mental computer by taking the following steps:

First, *define* your problem clearly, in writing. Your mind cannot go to work to bring you the right answer if the question itself is jumbled up and unclear. Exactly what is the problem? Why is it a problem? Could it be an opportunity in disguise? Is it a single problem, or is it a cluster problem—a problem made up of several smaller problems? Whichever it is, take some time to think it out and describe it clearly on paper so that you know exactly what you are dealing with. This is the beginning of the intuitive process.

Once you have a clear idea of the problem, ask yourself, "What *else* is the problem?" Are you dealing with a real problem, or are you simply dealing with a symptom of a deeper problem? Many people try to solve a work problem or a relationship problem without realizing that the *real* problem is that they are in the wrong job or relationship altogether.

There is an old saying, "There is a price that you can pay to be free of any problem, and you always know what it is." Your intuition will tell you the right thing to do, although the right thing may not be the easy or convenient thing. You must keep your mind open, in any case.

Gather Information

Once you have defined your problem clearly, begin to *research* and read and gather information about the problem. Has anyone else had this problem before you? What did he or she do about it? Don't try to reinvent the wheel. Sometimes a little research will turn up exactly the answer you are seeking. Try Google or Wikipedia.

For several months, two scientists at the IBM research laboratories in Zurich, Switzerland, had been working intensely on the problems of superconductivity. They knew what they were looking for but were making no progress, so they decided to take a break and come back to the problem later.

During the break, one of the scientists went down to the company library and, for a change of pace, began browsing through a French journal on ceramics. One of the articles told of a new ceramic application that had just been developed. It turned out to be exactly the key that the scientist had been looking for. He immediately took the article back to the laboratory, and by applying the described principle he and his partner discovered the secret of superconductivity. It was such an important scientific breakthrough that these two men were awarded the Nobel Prize in physics the following year.

Ask for Advice

Once you have defined your problem clearly and researched it as thoroughly as you can, speak to people who may have information that you can use. It's amazing how much you can learn simply by *asking questions* of others who may have had similar experiences. If you ask enough people, you can often find yourself in the position of being better informed than any one of the people giving you information could be acting in isolation.

A friend of mine, a management consultant, was employed by a large company to investigate the feasibility of placing a large sum of money in a particular type of real-estate investment. Company executives asked him to evaluate the possibilities nationwide and give them some advice on which direction to go.

First of all, he went online and downloaded copies of several articles that had been written in this field over the past few months. After reading the articles, he phoned some of the people and companies mentioned in the articles, and told them he was thinking of investing a large amount of money in this industry. He asked them for their insights and their ideas and what advice they would give.

Speak to Lots of People

Over the next few days he spoke to about thirty people in different parts of the country, all of whom specialized in this particular industry. Most of them were quite willing to give him whatever information he required, sometimes emailing it or sending it via FedEx®—because they looked upon him as a prospective investor.

By the time he was finished with his inquiries, he was one of the most well-informed people on this subject in the United States. He then summarized his findings and recommendations in a detailed report and submitted it to his client, along with a bill of $50,000 for consulting services. The client read the report and paid the bill willingly. And my friend the consultant went on to his next assignment.

Your Ability to Think

One of your most valuable assets is your *ability to think* and apply your mind toward getting results. The more you utilize your mental capabilities, by doing the things that other successful people do with their minds, the more successful and prosperous you will be, and the faster good things will happen for you.

Let's say that you have now defined your problem clearly, read and researched thoroughly, asked others for their advice and input, and written down every single detail of the problem or situation.

Once you have written out the details, go over them several times and let your mind *soak them up* so that your right brain is properly fueled to synthesize and integrate all the facts and respond intuitively. The very act of writing out all the details of a problem or opportunity often stimulates intuitive breakthroughs that lead to ideas and solutions that are superior to those currently being used.

Practice Mindstorming on Every Problem

If you still have no solution, your next step is to force yourself—discipline yourself—to *write out twenty ways* in which you think the problem could be solved. Begin by writing at the top of the page a question such as, How can I/we solve this problem or achieve this goal?

Then, quickly write out twenty solutions, or twenty answers, or twenty courses of action that might be possible. You can write more if you like, but twenty should be your minimum for this exercise. Often the twentieth answer contains the breakthrough you were looking for. Forcing yourself to think in this way will trigger your intuition and bring you an answer that will solve the situation perfectly.

For the rest of your career, whenever you have a big challenge, problem, or goal, write it as a question at the top of a page and then discipline yourself to generate at least twenty answers to it. This single exercise can change your life. It will electrify your intelligence. It will activate your creative mind so that it functions at a higher level all day long. It will actually make you smarter and increase your IQ. By practicing mindstorming on a regular basis, you make your mind stronger, faster, and more flexible than ever before. Just try it once. You will be amazed.

Forget About It

If you have followed the previous steps and still not come up with a solution that satisfies you, take the next step in intuitive decision-making, which is called *rumination* or *cerebration*. These words refer to the process of dropping all the information into your subconscious mind and then just forgetting about it for a while. Get your mind onto something else completely. During this period, your mind goes to work subconsciously to solve the problem while you are busy doing something else.

When they reach a dead end in problem solving or decision-making, many people find it helpful to turn the entire matter over to their subconscious mind and simply "ask" for an answer. A good time to do this is just before you go to sleep. Sometimes you will wake up in the morning with the answer springing full-blown into your mind. In other cases, so long as you keep your mind on other subjects, the answer will at a certain point emerge in its entirety, and you will know exactly what to do.

Recognizing an Intuitive Decision

How do you recognize an intuitive decision? How do you know that this is not simply a decision or solution that will lead to greater problems in the future? Well, there are four indicators that accompany every intuition-based solution or decision.

First of all, if the answer is truly from your intuition, it will be *complete* in every detail, answering every aspect of the problem, from beginning to end. The solution will integrate all of the various details and answer all of the concerns.

Second, an intuitive solution seems so simple that you wonder why you haven't thought of it before. It feels like a *blinding flash of the obvious.* You are amazed at how perfect it is, and you have the feeling that it was lying under your nose all the time.

The third indicator of an intuitive decision is that, whatever they are, the actions required are completely *within your capabilities* and resources. The solution will be something that you can do right now, with what you have, right where you are. You can act on it immediately.

The fourth indicator that it comes from your intuition is that the answer is accompanied by *a burst of joy and energy,* a feeling of elation that excites you. You will be eager to implement the solution.

Intuitive problem solving and decision-making is your key to the future. It is perhaps the most powerful faculty of your brain. And the regular use of your intuitive abilities will make them better, and stronger, and sharper, until you reach the point where you believe that there is really nothing that you cannot do if you put your mind to it. And you'll probably be right.

Action Exercises:

1. Identify the single biggest problem or obstacle holding you back from accomplishing your most important goal. Write it down.

2. Determine the cause of this problem. What *else* could be the cause?

3. Identify all the possible solutions. What else could be a solution?

4. If you still do not have a solution, practice mindstorming on the problem or goal and write out twenty possible solutions or answers.

5. Gather information. Ask other people. Seek answers on the Internet. Read everything you can.

6. If you still have not found the ideal answer, trust your intuition. Turn the problem over to your subconscious mind and get busy doing something else.

7. When the answer finally comes to you, take action immediately.

CHAPTER ELEVEN

Get Paid More and Promoted Faster

We cannot do great deeds unless we're willing to do
the small things that make up the sum of greatness.

—THEODORE ROOSEVELT

In this chapter, you will learn how to get paid more money for what you do and get promoted faster to higher levels of authority and responsibility.

These methods and techniques are used by the highest-paid and most successful people in our society. When you begin to use them yourself, you put your entire life and career onto the fast track. You will make more progress in the next couple of years than the average person makes in ten or twenty years of just plodding along with the crowd.

Dealing with Stress

How can you tell if you are in a situation that calls for zero-based thinking? It's simple. It's called *stress*. Whenever you experience chronic stress, unhappiness, anger, or dissatisfaction of any kind, it is almost always because you are in a situation that you wouldn't get into again if you had it to do over.

Apply zero-based thinking to your current job. Knowing what you now know, would you take this job again on the terms and conditions that you are now working under? Would you take this job working for this particular boss? Would you go to work for this company again? In this industry? At this salary? In this position?

If the answer is no, your next question is, How and how fast do I change this situation?

You can also apply zero-based thinking to every other part of your life. Especially you should apply it to your relationships.

The reason zero-based thinking is so important is that until you deal with the dissatisfactions of the present, you cannot move onward and upward to create the wonderful life that is possible for you in the future. Until you have the courage to face the unhappy realities of your current situation, you cannot move confidently forward in your career.

A Typical Story

My brother left high school and worked at odd jobs for a couple of years. Then he zero-based his work life and decided to change. After some thought about what he would really enjoy, he decided that he wanted to become a landscape architect. He spent the next three-and-a-half years' worth of nights and weekends in a technical school learning landscape architecture. He worked with landscape architects on the weekends and during the summer. Finally he got his degree.

At the age of twenty-seven, after two years designing gardens and yards, he used zero-based thinking again. He decided that landscape architecture was not for him. Instead he decided that he wanted to be a lawyer. He was now clear that the practice of law was the ideal career for him. It took him three more years of hard work in night school and on afternoons and weekends before he managed to get a degree in law. Today he has a thriving legal practice. He is doing work that he really enjoys and is making a wonderful living, earning what he's really worth.

The point it is this: you may have to put in a lot of effort and make a few false starts before you find the ideal career for you. But it all begins when you sit down and decide what it is you really want right now and then *get started*.

Make the Right Choices

Some industries are growing and expanding and absorbing many thousands of people. These industries are offering incredible opportunities, especially in high tech, for men and women who want to get ahead faster than the average person.

At the same time many other industries have flattened out or are actually declining. These industries are continually hiring to replace some of the workers that they are losing, but as a result of changes in the economy and consumer preferences, automation, technology, and competition, these industries are not likely to grow in the years ahead. Your task in seeking to earn what you are worth is to separate the high-growth industries from the low-growth industries.

Find a High-Growth Industry

You can make more progress toward getting paid more and getting promoted faster in a couple of years in a high-growth industry than you might in five or ten years in a slow-growth industry.

Once you have identified a high-growth industry, do your homework. Research and find out what companies in that industry are growing the most rapidly. Remember, 20 percent of the companies in any industry make 80 percent of the profits. They have better leadership, better products and services, better technology, and a better future. These are the companies where you want to work.

See yourself as a precious resource, like money, and see the market as a place where you are going to *invest yourself* to get the very highest return on your mental, emotional, and physical capital. Be perfectly selfish when it comes to committing your life and your work to a particular company in a particular industry.

Be Prepared to Change

A woman came up to me in one of my seminars recently and asked me what she could do to get paid more and promoted faster in her current job. I asked her what she was doing. She told me that she was working for a manufacturing company. As it happened, the company had tough competition from the Japanese, who offered the same products at lower prices but with equal or better quality. The company had not grown in ten years. I told her that there was very little future in a company or industry that was in decline. If she was really serious about getting ahead in her career and in her life, she should join a faster-growing company in a more dynamic industry.

She took my advice. She wrote to me a year later and told me that she had gotten a job with a high-tech company that was innovative and growing rapidly. She was now earning 40 percent more after one year with her new company than she had been earning after several years with the old company. Not only that, she had been promoted twice and was now on the fast track in her career.

Do Your Research

Remember the Harvard study that determined the most valuable asset that a company has is its *reputation*, or how it is known to its customers. If you are interested in working in a particular industry, ask around and find out which companies have the very best reputations for quality, service, innovation, and leadership. That is where you want to work.

Even within your own company, parts of the company are growing and expanding while other parts have leveled off or are declining in sales and profitability. Your goal must be to invest yourself in the part where a great future is possible for you.

The great oil billionaire J. Paul Getty, in his book *How to Be Rich*, recommends that you find a company that you want to work for, and that you then go to that company and be willing to take any job they will give you. Get your foot in the door. Once you are inside you will have a chance to perform and to move up rapidly. As they say, "Hitch your wagon to a star," and hold on!

Select the Right Boss

Choosing the right boss is one of the most important decisions that you ever make. It can accelerate your career and enable you get paid more and promoted faster than almost anything else you do.

You should look upon accepting a job as if you were entering into a marriage, with your boss as your spouse. He or she is going to have an enormous impact on how much you get paid, how much you enjoy your work, how rapidly you get promoted, and every other part of your work life.

When you are looking for a job, you should interview your potential boss carefully to make sure that he or she is the kind of person you would enjoy working with and for. This should be someone whom you would respect and look up to, someone who is friendly and supportive and on whom you can depend to help you move ahead as rapidly as possible.

Whenever possible, you should talk to other people who work for that boss. Check his or her background. Ask around and see if you can't find someone who knows the boss personally and who will give you a candid assessment of him or her.

Integrity Is the Key Quality

The very best bosses have certain specific qualities. First of all, they have *high integrity*. When they make a promise, they keep it. When they say they will do something, they do it exactly as they said. When they promise you a review or an increase, they follow through, right on schedule.

The best bosses are very clear when they describe a task to you. They are also *considerate and caring* about their employees. They are interested in you as a person as well as interested in you as an employee. They want to know about your personal life, your family, your spouse, and your children. They want to know about the things that concern you and that affect the way you think and feel at work.

This doesn't mean that a good boss is a confessor, or a nursemaid. But a good boss sees you as a whole person with a life apart from your work life.

You can always tell the quality of your relationship with your boss by how free you feel to speak honestly, openly, and directly to him or her about things that are bothering you. When you see your boss coming, you feel happy and comfortable rather than nervous or insecure. Perhaps the best measure of all is that when you are working with the right boss, you laugh a lot at work. You enjoy yourself, and you feel valuable and important as an employee and as a person.

Here is another place where you must practice zero-based thinking on a regular basis. Would you take this job, working for this boss, knowing what you now know, if you had it to do over?

If the answer is no, you must seriously consider changing your position and finding a boss whom you like and respect.

Be Prepared to Move

A friend of mine once found himself working for a critical and demanding boss in a medium-sized company. He liked the company; he liked the products and services that the company offered; he liked his coworkers. But his boss was causing him a lot of unhappiness. So he looked around within the company and selected a boss who was completely different. He then arranged to transfer out of his department and into the department where he would be working under the better boss. This decision changed his career completely.

As a result of working under a great boss, my friend performed at his very best. He was paid more and promoted faster, and in two years he was a manager himself and earning much more than he could ever have earned under the other boss.

Develop a Positive Attitude

Fully 85 percent of your success in work, no matter how intelligent or skilled you are, is going to be determined by your attitude and your personality. Your overall success, how much you are paid, and how fast you are promoted will be largely determined by how much people like you and want to help you.

Dr. Daniel Goleman of Harvard has written several books on the subject of emotional intelligence. His conclusion is that your emotional intelligence, or EI, is more important than your IQ in determining how successful you are in the world of work.

People who are *positive*, *cheerful*, and *optimistic* are always more liked and valued than people who are critical, pessimistic, and negative. One of the most critical determinants of your success in your career will be how well you perform as a part of a team. And your attitude will determine how good a team player you are at every stage of your career.

Working Well with Others

The very best team players are those who are cheerful, positive, and supportive of others. They have high levels of empathy and consideration. They are the kind of people whom others want to be around and to help.

Research shows that a positive, cheerful person is more likely to be paid more and promoted faster. This kind of person is more readily noticed by superiors who can accelerate his or her career. In addition, a positive person is supported by his or her coworkers and staff. There seems to be an upward pressure from his or her peers that drives a positive person forward at a faster rate.

The critical determinant of a positive attitude is how well you function under stress. Anyone can be positive when things are going well. But it is when you face difficulties and setbacks that you demonstrate to yourself and to everyone else what you are really made of. You've heard it said that "When the going gets tough, the tough get going."

A person with a positive attitude looks for the good in every person and every situation. He or she looks for something positive or humorous. The positive person tends to be constructive rather than destructive. And the good news is that a positive attitude is something that you can learn by practicing it, every single day, especially when it is most needed.

Create a Positive Image

It is absolutely amazing how many people are held back, year after year, because no one has ever taken them aside and told them how important their *external appearance* is to getting paid what they are truly worth.

I have personally studied the importance of image in business for many years. I have read dozens of books and articles and taught thousands of people. I can tell you with great assurance that how you look is going to have a major effect on how far you go and how fast you get there.

The first rule is that you should always *dress for success* in your job and in your company. Look at the top people in your industry. Look at the top people in your company. Look at the pictures in newspapers and magazines of the men and women who are being promoted to positions of higher responsibility and pay. Pattern yourself after the leaders, not the followers.

There are specific colors and color combinations that are more acceptable than others in business. Buy a good book on professional image, read it from cover to cover, and then follow its recommendations in your career.

Dress Like a Person with a Future

There is a lot of talk today about casual dress. It turns out that the people who are allowed to dress casually at work are back-office people. They are not people who deal face-to-face with customers. They are not people upon whom the future of the company depends. Even in Silicon Valley, where it is a badge of honor to dress down completely, the young executives keep tailored suits in their offices, which they put on when they are visited by a customer or an investment banker. They know the importance of dress.

If you are a person with a future, don't dress like a person without one. Dress like you are going somewhere in your life. And if everyone around you decides upon casual dress, this is all the better for you. You will stand out and look better to everyone who can have a positive influence on your career.

Remember, companies want to be proud of the employees that they introduce to their customers and their bankers. You must look like the kind of person an executive would be proud to introduce to another executive as a representative of the company.

Your First Impression

People judge you in the *first four seconds.* They will then grant you approximately thirty seconds more before they make a final decision and store this judgment away in their subconscious mind. After that it is very hard for a person to change his or her first impression of you. And you never get a second chance to make a good first impression.

Fully 95 percent of the first impression you make will be determined by your clothes. This is because your clothes cover fully 95 percent of your body, even on a hot day.

Always strive to look like a winner at work. Look like a valuable and important person. Look like a person with a great future who is going somewhere with this company. The rule is that you should spend twice as much on your clothes and buy half as many. No matter what anyone says, human beings are very strongly affected by the dress of other people. Your goal is to dress so that you look excellent in every business situation.

Watch Your Grooming

Your *grooming* is very important as well. One of my clients came to me for advice after many months of frustration in working with a customer of his company. I told him that his image was such that he did not appear trustworthy or credible to the customer. He wore a full beard that covered much of his face. He was a nice guy, but he was tripping himself up by the way he appeared.

He asked me specifically what he should change. I told him that, according to thousands of interviews, a beard is viewed as a mask, suggesting that the person has something to hide. "Shave it off," I told him.

He was shocked. He had been wearing the beard for years. Nonetheless he followed my advice, shaved his beard completely, and went back to see the customer again on Monday morning.

The customer's response to him was so totally different that my client was amazed. In fact, after six months of having gone back and forth, the customer signed a major agreement and gave my client a check right there for $30,000 to seal the contract, just one day after he changed his grooming.

You are a wonderful person with a wonderful future in front of you. It is important that everyone who sees you recognizes this fact in the first four seconds.

Start Earlier, Work Harder, and Stay Later

Develop a *workaholic mentality*. There is nothing that will bring you to the attention of the important people in your work life faster than for you to get a reputation as a hard, hard worker.

Everybody knows who the hard workers are in every business. The hardest workers are always the most respected in any company of value. They are always paid more and promoted faster for a very simple reason: they are more productive. They get more work done in a shorter period of time. They are more valuable to the company. They set a better example, and are the kind of people bosses are proud of and want to keep more than anyone else.

The rule is that *two extra hours* of work each day are all you really need to invest to become one of the most successful people of your generation. You can get these extra two hours by coming in an hour earlier and staying an hour later. In most cases, this will expand your day slightly but it will expand your career tremendously. You can also gain extra productive time by working through lunch. You don't have to follow the daily ritual of the average employee, who shuts down completely for thirty to sixty minutes in the middle of each day. This is not for you.

Work Longer Hours

The top people in every field work more hours than average people. In fact, the top 10 percent of money-earners in the United States work fifty to sixty hours per week. In addition, remember that they *work all the time they work*. They do not waste time. When they arrive at work early, they immediately start in on important tasks. They work steadily throughout the day. They are friendly, but they do not make small talk or chitchat with their coworkers.

This must be your goal as well. Work all the time you work. Do not play on the computer all day, make personal phone calls, read the newspaper, or chat about the latest football game or television program. Work all the time you work.

The average person today works at less than 50 percent of capacity. The other 50 percent is spent in idle socializing, personal phone calls, personal business, starting late, leaving early, and taking extended coffee breaks and lunch hours. Only about 5 percent of people in the world of work today actually work the whole time. Everyone else is functioning somewhere below their potential, in many cases far, far below.

Win the Contest

Imagine that your company is going to bring in an outside firm to assess all staff, to determine who works the hardest all the way through to who works the least hard. The winner is going to be paid more and promoted to a more important job. But here is the best part: only *you* know about this study. None of your coworkers will know what the outside firm is measuring.

Your goal is to win this contest. Your job is to be ranked as the hardest-working person in the entire company within twelve months. This goal will help you to get paid more and promoted faster than almost anything else you can possibly do. And *you* are the only person who can stop you from winning this contest.

The average working person today only puts in about thirty-two hours per week, after all coffee breaks, lunches, and traveling time have been deducted. In these thirty-two hours, the average employee produces only an average amount of work. The wages and salaries paid are eventually watered down to compensate for the low level of productivity that is being achieved.

But this is not for you. When you start work, hit the ground running. Avoid time-wasting activities, and especially time-wasting people.

Get Back to Work

When someone tries to distract you from what you are doing, smile cheerfully and say, "Well, I've got to get back to work!"

Keep repeating these words, over and over. "Back to work! Back to work! Back to work!"

If people want to talk or shoot the breeze, tell them that you have to get "back to work!" and that you would be pleased to chat with them at the end of the day. In most cases, they will never come back.

The fact is that life is a *contest*. You are in competition with everyone else who wants to be paid more and promoted faster. There is a race on and you are in it. Your job is to move yourself into the pole position and get ahead faster than anyone else.

Push to the Front

Fortunately there are proven and tested ways to come out ahead. One of the most important is for you to continually *ask for more responsibility*. Volunteer for every assignment. Go to your boss at least once every week and ask him or her for more responsibility.

I stumbled onto this method of rapid promotion many years ago when I was working for the chairman of a large conglomerate. Every week I would finish all my work and then go to him and ask him for more responsibility. For the first few weeks he only said that he would think about it. One day, after I had again asked for more work, he asked me if I would perform a particular task for him "when I got around to it."

This was my chance! It was Friday night, and he had asked me for a complete analysis of an investment the company was considering. I immediately went to work. I worked Friday evening and all day Saturday and Sunday. On Monday morning I came in early and got one of the secretaries to type up the report so that it looked great. Then I waited.

At ten thirty that Monday morning, the chairman called my office and asked me if there was any way that I could get him the numbers that he had requested on Friday. The bank had called and unexpectedly asked him for the details early so they could make a decision.

I went straight to his office with the report and laid it down on his desk. He picked up the phone and called the bank and closed a major loan as a result of it. From then on I started to get responsibility after responsibility and my entire future in that company changed.

Promote Yourself

Most people in the world of work do only what is asked of them. But this is not for you. Your job is to keep asking for more, and, whenever you are given a new responsibility, to fulfill it *quickly and well.* Remember: you want to develop a reputation for being the kind of person who is given the responsibility whenever someone wants to get something done quickly.

Do you want a promotion? Getting one is very much under your control. The fact is that you promote *yourself* every time you take on a new responsibility. You will eventually rise to the level of the responsibility you are willing to accept. There are no limits.

And there are fewer things more important in helping you get paid what you're really worth than for you to develop a reputation for *speed and dependability.* Be the kind of person your boss can count on to get the job done fast. Whatever it takes, treat every assignment you receive as if it were a test upon which your future career depended.

Seize Upon Every Opportunity

A young man in a large company told me this story: One year he volunteered to head up the United Way campaign in his company. All of the other managers had avoided this responsibility because it was so time-consuming.

But the young man saw it as an opportunity to perform for senior people in the company. He leaped at the responsibility, and did an outstanding job of getting everyone in the company to contribute to making the campaign a success. In the course of running the campaign, the young man was able to meet with almost every senior manager in the company, getting a chance to talk to them and become known by them.

As a result of the success of the campaign, the president of the company was given a special award and was written up in the newspapers as one of the top executives in the community. Within six months after the campaign ended, this young man had been promoted twice. A year later, his former manager, who had avoided the United Way responsibility, was working for my friend.

Ask for What You Want

This is one of the most important success principles you will ever learn to help put your career onto the fast track: *the future belongs to the askers.* The future does not belong to those people who sit back, wishing and hoping that their lives and their work will become better. The future belongs to those people who step up and ask for what they want. If they don't get it, they ask again and again until they do.

Ask your boss what you have to do to qualify for an increase. There is no point in your working hard if you don't know exactly what it is that you have to do to get paid more and promoted faster. Clarity is essential. Go to your boss and ask, and ask again if you are still not clear.

Ask for an Increase in Pay

If you want an increase, you must ask for it. And the way you ask is by building a case, as a lawyer would build a case, for your getting the amount that you want to receive. Instead of saying that you need more money, as most people do, you have a different strategy. You put together a list of the jobs that you are now doing and the additional experience and skills you have developed. Show the financial impact of your work on the overall operations of the company and the contribution that you are making as a top employee.

Present this information to your boss, in writing, and tell him or her that, based on all of this, you would like an increase of a specific amount of money per month and per year. In many cases, you will get the increase simply by asking for it in an intelligent way. In some cases you will get less than you requested. If this happens, ask what you will have to do to get the rest of the increase that you asked for.

If your request for an increase is turned down, ask exactly what you will have to do to get the increase you requested at a later time and exactly when that increase will be payable. Be specific. Be clear. And don't be afraid to ask.

Never Fear Rejection

The question of asking is a major challenge in human relations today. People are afraid to ask because they fear rejection. They fear being told no. But think about it this way: before you ask, you have nothing. If you ask and the person tells you no, you are in exactly the same position that you were in before. But in many cases, the person will say yes, and then your whole future can be different.

Sometimes people are afraid to ask because they feel that they don't deserve it. They feel that they are not good enough to be paid more than they are currently receiving. But an interesting thing happens when you begin asking for what you want: you actually begin to feel more deserving and more valuable. You begin to think in terms of *why* you are entitled to the money rather than in terms of *why not*.

If you are not happy with your current job, ask to be transferred to a different job. If you are not happy with the way you are being treated, ask to be treated differently. If you are not happy with any part of your work life, ask for it to be changed.

Of course, you should ask politely. Ask in a warm and friendly way. Ask cheerfully. Ask expectantly. Ask confidently. And ask persistently, if necessary. But be sure to ask. The future belongs to the askers, and the more you ask for the things you want, the more likely you are to get them. Just try it once and you will be amazed.

Plan Your Strategy in Advance

Once I had a secretary working for me named Diane. Diane had been fired from a bank for some reason and very much needed a job. I hired her for $800 per month (this was back in 1987). After two months, because she was doing a good job, I increased her salary to $1,000 per month, which was still quite low. And after two more months I increased her salary to $1,200 per month. As you can calculate, this was a 50 percent increase in a very short time.

After Diane had been working for me for about six months, she told me she would like to talk to me about her compensation. We arranged a time where we sat down, closed the door, and discussed her pay. She told me that she had been thinking about her salary and that she would like an increase.

I had expected this, and I offered her another $200 per month, raising her salary to $1,400 per month. She thanked me for the thought and told me that she had done a good deal of research in the marketplace and had concluded that a person of her skills and abilities was worth $1,800 per month. That was the amount that she wanted.

Not Afraid to Ask

I was surprised. I sat there looking at her, and she stared back at me without blinking. Then I thought about how quickly she had learned every detail of my business. She had taken additional computer courses so that she could handle the bookkeeping and word processing. She had introduced herself to our customers and was handling customer-service problems. She had gone to work to make herself more valuable in every area. And I realized that she was worth the extra money. To replace her I would have to pay as much, if not more, to someone else. I agreed to her request and gave her the increase of $600 per month. She thanked me with a big smile and went back to work. I just sat there shaking my head.

Here's the point: not only did Diane do everything exactly right, but she carefully prepared her timing and her request. Then she stepped up and asked for exactly what she wanted, giving good, solid reasons for a 50 percent increase in pay.

For the rest of your career, you must develop the habit of asking for what you want on every occasion. Ask at the beginning of the job, ask in the middle, and ask at every stage. Ask for more responsibilities, ask for more money. Ask for more rapid advancement. But be sure to *ask*.

Guard Your Integrity as a Sacred Thing

Your character is your most valuable personal asset. It is the critical factor that others use when evaluating you for more pay or more rapid promotion.

The key to character is *truthfulness*. No matter what, always tell the truth, in every situation. When you give your word, keep it. When you make a promise, fulfill it. When you say you'll do something, no matter what it costs, be sure to do it.

As I've said, another important part of character is *loyalty*. Lack of loyalty is a fatal mistake to make in business. When you are loyal, you never complain about, condemn, or criticize your company, your boss, your products, your services, or anything else about your work. Even if you are unhappy for some reason, you keep it to yourself. You always support the people you work with, and you demonstrate complete loyalty to the person who signs your paycheck.

Shakespeare once wrote, "To thine own self be true, And it must follow, as the night the day, Thou canst then not be false to any man."

Be true to yourself and then be true to everyone around you. Always live in truth with yourself and with others. Never compromise your integrity for anything.

The good news is that when you live with complete integrity, inside and outside, you feel *wonderful* about yourself. You have greater self-confidence and higher self-esteem. You feel positive and powerful. And most of all, you earn the respect, trust, and loyalty of all the people around you. Always guard your integrity as a sacred thing.

Be Future-Oriented in Your Work and Personal Life

Future-orientation requires that you develop a *long-term vision* for yourself and your career. Dr. Edward Banfield's work at Harvard over a fifty-year period concluded that the most successful men and women in our society have "longtime perspective." They think ten and twenty years into the future, and they make their decisions each day based on this long time horizon. And so should you.

The most important word in future-orientation is the word *idealization*. This requires that you idealize or imagine your ideal future career in every respect. Project yourself forward three to five years, and imagine that your life is perfect and that you are doing exactly the right job for you.

If your work situation were perfect, what would it look like? What would you be doing? How much would you be earning? With whom would you be working? Where would you be working?

Once you have idealized your perfect job, ask yourself about the kind of person you would need to become to get and keep that job. What kind of skills would you have? How high up would you be in your field? What new talents and abilities would you have to tap into and develop?

What Is the Gap?

Practice what is called Gap Analysis on your job. Look at the difference between where you are today and where you would like to be in the future. Where is the gap? What changes should you begin making, right now, to prepare yourself for the kind of job you want? As Abraham Lincoln said, "The best way to predict the future is to *create* it."

One of the qualities of leaders in every field is that they think about the future much of the time. It is important that you think about the future as well, because that is where you are going to spend the rest of your life. And the more you think about the future, the more optimistic and positive you become. The more you develop a clear vision of where you want to be in the years ahead, the more likely it is that you will take the steps, each day, to make your vision into your reality.

Think about the future of your company as well. Look at the cycles and trends in your business. Think about where your company is going and what your company needs to do to be successful in the future. What can you do to help?

The more future-oriented you are in your position, the more you will be paid and the more rapidly you will be promoted. The more future-oriented you are, the better decisions you will make and the more positive impact you will have on your company's operations. The more future-oriented you are, the more you will feel in control of your life, your career, and your personal destiny.

Become Goal-Oriented in Everything You Do

People who have clear, written goals and who know exactly what they want in each area of their lives accomplish vastly more than people who are not sure or who are unclear about what they want.

Perhaps nothing can help you more in your attempts to be paid more and promoted faster than for you to become an intensely goal-oriented person. Fortunately, the skill of setting and achieving goals is something that you can learn quite quickly and then develop through practice, day after day. (The seven-step method for goal-setting and -achieving is described earlier, beginning on page 130.)

The more goal-oriented you are at work, the more results you will get and the more valuable you will become. When you become intensely goal-oriented, you will use your time better and stand out from the others. You will attract more opportunities for greater responsibilities. By becoming intensely goal-oriented, you will inevitably get paid more and promoted faster.

Become Intensely Results-Oriented

Your ability to get results is the most important single determinant of how much you are paid and how rapidly you are promoted. In business, results are everything. It has been determined that within two years of your leaving college or school, your education has ceased to have much impact on your career. From that point on, all that matters is your ability to *perform* and *get results* for your company.

Many people start off with limited education and few skills. But by focusing on results single-mindedly, they can accomplish vastly more than people with excellent educations and many advantages. This must be your strategy as well.

Get Your Boss on the Same Page

Make a list of everything you feel that you have been hired to accomplish, take it to your boss, and ask your boss to organize the list according to his or her priorities. What does he or she consider to be more important or less important on your list? From then on, always work on whatever task your boss considers to be more important than anything else.

There is no better way to get paid more and promoted faster than for you to be working, all day long, on the tasks that are of greatest concern to your boss. All of the best days of your working life will be when you are working on what your boss considers most important. And the good news is that the more that you accomplish important tasks, the more important tasks you will be given to accomplish.

The Value of Mentors

Benjamin Franklin once said, "There are two ways to acquire wisdom; you can either buy it or borrow it. By buying it, you pay full price in terms of time and cost to learn the lessons you need to learn. By borrowing it, you go to those men and women who have already paid the price to learn the lessons and get their wisdom from them."

This is the essence of the mentor-mentee relationship. By going to people who are ahead of you in the personal or professional arena, and by opening yourself up to their input, advice, and guidance, you can save yourself the many months (or maybe even years) and the thousands of dollars it would cost to learn what you need to learn all by yourself.

Proven Success Methods

Kop Kopmeyer, a famous success authority, said that one of the most important secrets of success is to *learn proven success methods*. He once told me that perhaps the fastest way to get ahead was to study the experts and do what they do, rather than try to learn it all yourself. He said that no one lives long enough to learn everything he or she needs to learn starting from scratch. To be successful, we absolutely, positively have to find people who have already paid the price to learn the things that we need to learn to achieve our goals.

The mentors you choose should be people you respect, admire, and want to be like. The advice you seek should be guidance regarding your character and personality and specific ideas on how you can do your job better and faster. Remember, you can't figure it all out for yourself. You have to have the help of others. You have to find men and women who will guide you and advise you on the road of life, or else you will take a long, long time getting anywhere.

Character and Competence

There are two vital aspects to look for in a mentor: the first is character and the second is competence.

Character is by far the more important. Look for a mentor who has the kind of character you admire and respect. Look for a person who has a high degree of intelligence, integrity, judgment, and wisdom. The more you associate, even in your mind, with men and women who are advanced in the development of their character, the more you will tend to pattern them and become like them.

The second thing you look for in a mentor is competence. This means that the person is extremely good at what he or she does. A good mentor in your career is one who has the knowledge, skills, and abilities to move ahead far more rapidly than his or her peers.

Your Degree of Openness

The impact of a mentor on your life is dependent on two additional factors. The first is your degree of openness to being influenced by another person. Openness is so important because many people, especially young people, are extremely impatient, always looking for shortcuts. When they get advice that another person has spent many years learning the basis for, they often try to add their own variations and improve on it without ever having mastered the original instruction in the first place.

Remember, when you open yourself up to guidance and input from another person, concentrate first on understanding and learning exactly what that person has to teach you. Afterward you can modify the lesson to suit your changing circumstances.

The Willingness to Help

The second factor that determines the influence of a mentor on your life is the willingness of the mentor to help you improve in your career and achieve your personal goals. We know that the more emotionally involved someone is in our life, the more susceptible we are to being influenced by that person. When you consciously and deliberately seek out a mentor, you must look for someone who genuinely cares about you as a person and who really wants you to be successful in your endeavors.

For a good mentor-mentee relationship, you must be open to the influence and instruction of your mentor, and at the same time your mentor must be genuinely concerned about your well-being and your ultimate success. These are the two essentials.

Over the course of your life and career, you can have several mentor-mentee relationships. As you grow and develop, you will move on to mentors who can give you the kind of advice that is most effective for your current situation.

The most wonderful thing about this process is that successful people are very open to helping other people who want to be successful. This is especially true if you yourself are willing to be a mentor to those who are younger and less experienced than you. The more open you are to helping others up the ladder of success, the more open others will be to helping you.

The fastest way for you to succeed is by piggybacking on the good advice and counsel of men and women who have already spent years learning how to succeed. When you do this on a regular and systematic basis, you will open up doors of opportunity and possibilities for yourself that today you cannot even imagine.

Here are seven actions you can take to find, keep, and get the very most benefit from a mentor:

1. Set clear goals for yourself in your career. Know exactly what it is you want to accomplish before you start thinking of the type of person who can help you accomplish it.

2. Work, study, and practice continually to get better and better at what you do. The very best mentors are only interested in helping you if they feel it is going to be of value. You will have no problem attracting people to you when you develop a reputation for being an up-and-coming person in your field.

3. When you find a potential mentor, don't ask for too much time or make a nuisance of yourself. Instead, ask for ten minutes of his or her time, in person, in private—nothing more. Remember, most mentors are busy people, and they may be opposed to someone trying to take up a lot of their time. This is not personal.

4. When you meet with a potential mentor, express your desire to be more successful in your field. Tell him or her that you would very much appreciate a little guidance and advice to help you move ahead. Ask for an answer to a specific question, or for a specific book or audio-program recommendation, or for a specific idea that has been helpful to him or her in the past. Whatever advice or guidance he or she gives you, take action on it immediately.

5. After the initial meeting, send a thank-you note, and express your gratitude and appreciation for his or her time and guidance. Mention that you hope to meet again if you have another question.

6. Each month, drop your mentor a short note telling him or her about what you are doing and how you are progressing. There is nothing that makes a potential mentor more open to helping you than your making it clear that the help is doing you some good.

7. Arrange to meet with your mentor again, perhaps on a monthly basis, or even more often if you work closely together.

Become Idea-Oriented in Your Work

Always look for better, faster, cheaper, easier ways to get the job done and achieve the desired result.

The good news is this: you are a potential *genius*! You have more natural intelligence and creativity than you have ever used up to now. The more you use your ability to generate ideas, the smarter and more creative you become, and the more and better ideas you come up with to use in every part of your work.

The most successful people in every business are those who are always coming up with new and better ideas, new and better ways to achieve the goals of the company. No one is smarter than you. No one is better than you. No one has more natural creativity than you, just as no one has more muscles than or different muscles from you. It is all a matter of how often you use your creative muscles in your life and your work.

The more ideas you come up with to improve sales, reduce costs, or increase the profitability of your business, the more you will be paid and the faster you will be promoted.

Develop Intense People-Orientation

Relationships are everything in both work and personal life. Your level of success, your rate of promotion, and your pay will be largely determined by how well you get along with the important people in your life. Your future will be largely determined by the number of people you know and who know you in a positive way.

Birds of a feather flock together. People like to pay and promote people whom they like and feel comfortable with. The more people like you and enjoy your company, the more doors they will open for you and the more obstacles they will remove from your path.

A recent study found that during economic downturns, companies were much more likely to lay off people with negative personalities, even if those people were technically superior to others. Over a twenty-year period, the study's researchers found that fully 95 percent of people who were let go by their companies were let go because of personality problems. Poor social skills are the number one obstacle to getting paid more and promoted faster.

The key to becoming a people-oriented person is to practice the *golden rule* in everything you do. Treat other people the way you would like them to treat you. Offer to help other people to do their jobs whenever you see an opportunity. Practice being courteous, kind, and considerate when you deal with other people, especially people whose positions pay less than your own. Thomas Carlyle once said, "A great man shows his greatness by the way he treats little men."

Broaden Your Network

Expand your network of contacts in every way possible. Join your local business associations, and attend every business function related to your field. Introduce yourself to other people and find out what they do. Ask good questions and listen carefully to the answers. Build your network of contacts wider and wider so that you are eventually known to a great number of the key people in your industry.

Many people have transformed their careers by getting to know other key people in the business community. When a position comes open, the well-connected person is remembered and offered an opportunity to interview and, eventually, to get the job. Many people have gone from doing a good job at one place to becoming a senior executive with higher pay and stock options at another place just because of a contact or friendship that developed at a business or association meeting.

An Attitude of Gratitude

In your work, practice being a friendly, helpful, and cheerful person. Express gratitude to people on every occasion. Say thank you to anyone who does anything for you, large or small. As I've said, go out of your way to compliment people on their traits, possessions, or accomplishments. As Abraham Lincoln wrote, "Everybody likes a compliment."

Treat each person in your company as if he or she were one of the most valuable customers of the business. Treat your boss, your coworkers, and your staff all as valuable and important people. When you make other people feel important, they will look for every opportunity to make you feel important as well. And when you are liked and respected by all the people around you, all kinds of opportunities will open up for you to be paid more and promoted faster.

Be Growth-Oriented

Dedicate yourself to lifelong learning. Set yourself apart from the crowd by being the person in the company who is learning and growing at a faster rate than anyone else.

The fact is that most of your knowledge and skill today has a half-life of about two and a half years. This means that within five years most of what you know today will be obsolete or irrelevant. In order to survive and thrive in the fast-changing world of tomorrow, you will have to continually upgrade your knowledge and skills at a faster and faster rate just to stay even, much less to get ahead.

The highest-paid 10 percent of Americans read two to three hours each day in their fields, just to keep current. They are continually taking in information from every possible source. As we move at hyperspeed through the information age, the top people in every business realize that they must stay ahead of the wave of change or they will be bowled over by it.

Today, you have a very simple choice. You can be a *master* of change, or you can be a *victim* of change. There is very little middle ground. Your job is to be a master of change, by continually learning to be better and better at what you do.

Continual Learning

We have moved today from the era of manpower to the era of mind power. We have moved from the use of physical muscles to the use of mental muscles. Today the chief sources of value in our society are knowledge and the ability to apply it in a timely fashion. In the information age, knowledge is king, and those people who develop the ability to continually acquire new and better forms of knowledge—which they then can apply to their work and their lives—will be the movers and shakers in our society for the indefinite future.

When you learn and practice the techniques for rapid learning, when you join the learning revolution, you will learn how to unlock the incredible powers of your mind. You will learn how to become smarter faster than ever before. You will learn how to become a master of your fate rather than a victim of circumstances. You will learn how to take complete control of your present and future so that you can accomplish and achieve anything you want in life.

Knowledge is doubling every two to three years in almost every occupation and profession, including yours. This means that your knowledge must double every two to three years for you to just stay even. People who are not aggressively and continually upgrading their knowledge and skills are not staying in the same place. They are falling behind.

The Consequences of Not Learning

You see the failure to learn and grow all around you, in massive layoffs, declining wages, and growing insecurity in the workforce. You see it in the increasing bewilderment and despair on the part of people who are being displaced from low-skill jobs that have either moved overseas or disappeared altogether. We are in the midst of a societal revolution where unionized industrial workers are becoming a smaller and smaller percentage of our workforce each year.

As recently as the '50s and '60s it was common to believe that you would finish your schooling, get a job with a large company, and stay with that company for the rest of your life.

Today, with workforce requirements changing so rapidly, you must continually be asking yourself, "What is my next job going to be?" You must also be asking yourself, on a regular basis, "What is my next career going to be?"

Imagine Starting Over

Imagine for a moment that your entire company or industry vanished overnight, and you had to start all over again in an entirely new business doing an entirely different job. What would it be? And don't think this question is hypothetical or that it only applies to someone else. It is a scenario that you will probably have to deal with, perhaps far sooner than you expect. In thinking about your new job and your new career, here is the most important question of all: "What will I have to be absolutely, positively *excellent* at doing, in order to earn a high income at my new job in my new career?"

In the world of work, the answer to almost every question, and the solution to almost every problem, is for you to learn and practice something new and different. You must maximize the incredible power of your brain to absorb and apply new ideas and information. Only in this way will you be able to lead the field and rise to the top of any profession or occupation.

The Educated Person

Management consultant Peter Drucker says that the truly educated person today is a person who has learned how to learn continually throughout life. Tom Peters says that continual learning may be the only real source of sustainable competitive advantage for individuals and corporations.

Peter Senge, who wrote *The Fifth Discipline*, says that only "learning organizations," those organizations that are capable of taking in new information, adapting it, and using it faster than their competitors, will survive in the fast-changing, competitive world of tomorrow.

The more you know, the better you will be at solving problems and getting the results for which people will pay you. The more you know, the more freedom and opportunity you will have. And the more you learn and the faster you learn it, the more rapidly you will move onward and upward in your career and in every other area of your life.

Bridge the Gap

Between where you are and where you want to go, there is almost always a gap, and in almost every case you will find that you can bridge this gap with new knowledge and more current skills. In order to get from where you are to where you have accomplished your goals, you have to learn and practice something new and different. You have to develop new skills and abilities. You have to learn new attitudes and methods. You have to learn new techniques and practices.

If you want to be a better parent, you must learn and practice better parenting skills. If you want to be a better spouse, you must study and practice relationship skills. If you want to earn more money, you have to determine what it is that people will pay more money for and then get busy learning and practicing those skills. There is no other way.

Learn How to Learn

Specific knowledge and specific skills will become obsolete with the passing of time, but *learning how to learn* is a permanent skill that you can use all the days of your life. The people who join the learning revolution and who learn how to learn faster, like those people who first learned how to operate computers or learned how to become excellent in their fields, will be able to earn more in one or two years of work than the average person earns in perhaps five or ten years.

By joining the learning revolution, you will enhance every area of your life. You will be able to help your spouse and your children unlock and realize more of their individual potential. You will be a better friend, in helping your friends use more of their abilities. And you will be a better manager, business owner, moneymaker, or salesperson by developing the skills that will enable you to get far more out of yourself *and* other people than ever before.

The Keys to Lifelong Learning

There are three keys to lifelong learning. The first is for you to read at least one hour every day in your chosen field. Reading is to the mind what exercise is to the body. If each day you read for one hour from a good book in your field, that will translate into about one book per week. One book per week will translate into roughly fifty books per year. Fifty books per year will translate into five hundred books over the next ten years. The very act of continually reading in your field will make you one of the best-informed and highest-paid people in your business in a very short time.

Enroll in Automobile University

The second key to continual learning is, as I've described before, for you to listen to audio programs in your car as you drive from place to place. You can become one of the best-educated and most competent people in your field by listening to educational audio programs rather than music in your car.

Travel Any Distance

The third key to continual learning is for you to take every course and seminar that you can find. The highest-paid people I know will actually travel from one side of the country to the other to take intense two- or three-day seminars that can help them in their careers.

A good book, audio program, or seminar can give you ideas and insights that can save you years of hard work in reaching the same level of income. From now on, become hungry for new knowledge. In the final analysis, nothing can help you to get paid more and promoted faster than becoming one of the most knowledgeable and competent people in your field.

Commit to Excellence

Resolve to be the best at what you do. Resolve today to join the top 10 percent of people in your field. Look around you at the top people and realize that no one is smarter than you, and no one is better than you. If they are ahead of you today, it is because they are doing things differently from you. And, as I've said, whatever anyone else has done, you can do as well, if you just learn how.

Let me also remind you that the way you become one of the best people in your field is to identify your Key Result Areas, the skill areas where you absolutely, positively have to do an excellent job in order to be successful in your field. Remember that there are seldom more than five to seven Key Result Areas in any job. Your ability to perform at an excellent level in each of these areas is the key determinant of how much you are paid and how fast you are promoted.

Once you have identified your Key Result Areas, ask yourself this key question: "What one skill, if I developed and performed it in an excellent fashion, would have the greatest positive impact on my career?"

This is perhaps the most important question you will ever ask and answer for your career. If you do not know which one skill can help you the most, go to your boss and ask him or her. Ask your coworkers. Ask your spouse. But whatever it takes, you absolutely must find out the one key skill that can help you the very most if you master it at a high level.

After that you set the acquisition of this skill as a goal; you write it down, you make a plan, and you work on it every single day. This simple exercise is so powerful that it alone can change your entire life.

In addition, set standards of excellent performance for yourself in everything you do. Develop a reputation for quality work. If you are a manager or supervisor, demand quality work from everyone who reports to you. Remember the old saying "Good enough seldom is."

In the end no one will care how fast you did the job. All they will care about is how *well* you did the job. Resolve to become absolutely excellent at what you do and then do your job in an absolutely excellent fashion. Set this as your standard and never compromise it for the rest of your career.

Become Customer-Oriented in Your Work

In a business, customers are everything. The primary purpose of a business is to *create and keep a customer.* Profits in a business are the result of creating and keeping customers in a sufficient number and at a reasonable cost.

Customers pay all salaries and wages. Customers determine the success or failure of companies and of everyone in them. Sam Walton once said, "There is only one boss. The customer. And he can fire everybody in the company from the chairman on down, simply by spending his money somewhere else."

Who are your customers? Who are your key customers? Who are your secondary customers? The definition of a customer is *someone who depends on you for the satisfaction of his or her needs or someone whom you depend upon for the satisfaction of your needs.*

Who Are Your Customers?

By this definition, your *boss* is your customer. Your ability to satisfy your boss largely determines your success in your career. Your *coworkers* are your customers. Without their active help and support, it is almost impossible for you to do your work well. Your *staff* are your customers. If they don't do what you require of them, the quality of your own work will suffer, and your position will be in jeopardy. And of course, the people who buy your products and services are your customers. Everyone is dependent on everyone else for something.

Your success in your life and your career will be totally determined by how well you serve and satisfy all the different customers around you. And the more and the better you satisfy your customers, the more customers you will be given to satisfy.

Four Levels of Customer Satisfaction

Let us focus here on your customers for the products and services you sell. There are four levels of customer satisfaction in the marketplace. The first is where you *meet customer expectations*. This is the minimum for survival. What do you have to do to meet the expectations of your customers? What are these expectations exactly?

The second level of customer satisfaction is where you *exceed customer expectations*. This requires that you do more than the customer expected. This is the key to the future. What can you do in every customer interaction to go beyond what the customer is expecting from you?

The third level of customer satisfaction is where you *delight your customers*, where you do something that causes them to light up with unexpected pleasure. What can you add to your products or your services that would make your customers brighten up with pleasure?

The highest level of customer satisfaction is where you *amaze your customers*, where you do things that make them so happy that not only do they want to buy from you again but they want to bring their friends to you as well.

Every single day, you should be looking for ways to exceed expectations and to both amaze and delight the customers that your company depends upon to survive and thrive. Your ability to serve and satisfy your customers will get you paid more and promoted faster than you can imagine.

Think About Profits All the Time

Contributing to company profits is vital for your future. This is the key to growth, to success, and to rapid promotion. The very best people in every organization are intensely focused on what they can do to increase the profitability of the company. And the greater effect your work can have on profitability, the more important you become, and the more you will be paid.

There are two ways to increase profitability in a company. The first is to increase revenues, by selling more of existing products and services or by developing new products and services that can be sold to more customers. The second way to increase profitability is to decrease the costs of providing products and services to the existing market. The very best goal for you is a combination: to be continually looking for ways to increase sales and revenues while at the same time reducing the costs of delivering those products and services.

The New Normal

Fully 80 percent of all products that will be in the market in five years do not exist today. The rate of turnover and change is extraordinary. You must constantly be looking for new products and services and new combinations of existing products and services that you can bring to the market to maintain and increase revenues for your organization. One good idea is all you need to change your entire career.

At the same time you should be looking for ways to reorganize, restructure, and reengineer every part of your work so that you can get the job done faster and at a lower cost than before. Squeeze out every extra penny of expense. Examine every single cost to see if it cannot be decreased or eliminated somehow. Many executives have found that they can cut the cost of producing a product or service by 50 percent, 60 percent, and 70 percent, while increasing the speed at which that product or service is brought to the market. This kind of improvement should be your goal as well.

The most important and highest-paid people in any organization are those most concerned with the overall profitability of the company. When you become a key player in affecting profitability in some way, you come immediately to the attention of the people who can most help you in your career. Your ability to increase profitability in some way is one of the very fastest ways for you to get paid more and promoted faster.

Develop Your Own Power Base

Power is a very real and important part of organizational and business life. Your ability to acquire and use power in your career is essential to your long-term success. Let me explain.

Power, in its simplest sense, means *control over people and resources*. Power means that you have the ability to influence things that are done or that are not done.

There are two major types of power: *positive* and *negative*. A person with positive power uses his or her influence to help the organization achieve more of its goals doing things faster, better, and cheaper. A person with negative power uses his or her position or influence to advance his or her own interests at the expense of the organization.

Three Forms of Power

There are three forms of power that you can develop. The first of these is called *expert power*. Expert power arises when you become very good at doing something that is important to the company. As a result of it people look up to you and respect you for the value of the contribution you can make.

The second form of power is called *ascribed power*. This comes to you when you are liked and admired because of your ability to be a team player, to get along well with others, to help others to achieve their goals and do their jobs. Ascribed power arises when people like you and want you to be successful. This form of power enables you to become more influential in your organization. Ascribed power comes from your attitude and your personality more than anything else.

Position Power

The third kind of power is *position power.* This is the power, authority, and ability to reward and punish that goes along with a specific title. Every title or position has some of this power attached to it.

The good news is that as you develop expert power and ascribed power, you will be given position power. The people above you and around you will want you to be in a position of greater influence because you have demonstrated that the more influence you have, the more and better results you can get for the company. Position power is the very best and most important of all powers for you to develop and build.

And the more you acquire and use your power in a positive and constructive way, the more power you will attract to yourself. More people around you will support you and help you. The people above you will give you more resources. You will be more respected and esteemed by others. And you will definitely be paid more and promoted faster.

Become Intensely Action-Oriented

As I've said, action-orientation is the most outwardly identifiable quality of a top-performing man or woman. He or she is extremely action-oriented. He or she is constantly in motion. He or she is always doing something that is moving the company toward the achievement of its goals.

Remember: resolve today to develop a sense of urgency. Develop a bias for action. Develop a fast tempo in everything you do.

The good news is that the faster you move, the more things you get done. The more you get done, the more experience you acquire, and the more competent you become. The faster you move, the more energy you have. The faster you move, the more results you get, and the more valuable you become to your company and to everyone around you.

Develop a Sense of Urgency

Only 2 percent of people in our society have a sense of urgency. And these 2 percent are the people who eventually rise to the top of every organization. When you develop a reputation for *speed and dependability* in everything you do, you attract to yourself more and more opportunities to do more and more things of greater and greater importance, faster and faster.

An average person with an average background who moves quickly when opportunity arises will eventually run circles around a genius who moves slowly. Working quickly will open more doors for you and get you paid more and promoted faster than almost anything else you can possibly do.

Today the primary source of wealth is *talent and ability*. All of the money and resources flow to the men and women who demonstrate that they can get the job done and get it done quickly. When you begin to practice these different ways to get paid more and promoted faster, you will put your career onto the fast track. You will move ahead more rapidly than anyone else around you. You will move upward and onward and you will make your life and career into something truly extraordinary.

Action Exercises:

1. See yourself as a valuable person with unlimited potential for career success and achievement. What goals would you set for yourself if you were *guaranteed* of success?

2. Make a plan for continual, lifelong personal and professional development. Get a book or audio program today and get started.

3. Look at yourself in the mirror and ask, "Do I look like one of the highest-paid people in my business?" If the answer is no, then the next step is for you to make some changes.

4. Determine what specific activities you could engage in immediately to increase your value and contribution to your business.

5. Begin today to develop your power base in your business by becoming very good at what you do.

6. Select at least one person whom you would like to have as a mentor and approach that person in the way described in this chapter.

7. Make it a lifelong habit to ask for more responsibility, and when you get it, to do the job quickly and well, thereby promoting *yourself.*

CHAPTER TWELVE

Perception Is Everything

We must all suffer from one of two pains: the pain of
discipline or the pain of regret. The difference is that
discipline weighs ounces while regret weighs tons.

—JIM ROHN

Have you noticed that some people receive more promotions
and greater pay than their colleagues, even though they don't
seem to be more competent or capable than others? This doesn't
seem fair. Why should some people get ahead while others, who
seem to be working just as hard, and sometimes even harder,
get passed over for promotion and the additional rewards that
go with it?

The fact is that to be a great success, it is important not only to
be good at what you do, but also to be *perceived* as being good at
what you do. Human beings are creatures of perception. It is not
what they see but what they think they see that determines how
they think and act.

If your coworker is perceived as being more promotable than you are, for whatever reasons, then it is very likely that your coworker will get additional responsibilities and more money, even though you know that you could do a better job if given the chance.

Supercharging Your Career

Fortunately, however, there are several things that you can do to increase your visibility and accelerate the speed at which you move ahead in your career.

The starting point of attaining higher visibility is for you to develop a high level of competence, to become very good at the most important things you do. Determine what parts of your job are most important to your boss and to your company, and then make the decision to become excellent in those areas.

To stand out, you must be perceived as being very good at what you do. Your future depends on it. This perception alone will bring you to the attention of key people faster than you can imagine. The perception of excellent performance will open up opportunities for greater responsibilities, higher pay, and better positions. Becoming good at what you do should be the foundation of your strategy for gaining higher visibility and rapid advancement in your career.

Employers everywhere are looking for men and women of *action*, people who will get in there and get the job done right and as soon as possible. When you develop a reputation for competence and the predictable delivery of results, you quickly become visible to all the key people in your working environment.

Look the Part of Success

Excellence at what you do is essential, but it's not enough. There are additional elements that go into the perception that others have of you. And one of the most important elements is your overall image, from head to toe. How you appear to others makes a real difference.

As I've described, a recent survey of personnel executives found that the decision to hire or not hire is made in the first *thirty seconds.* Many people believe that the decision to accept or reject a job candidate is actually made in the first *four* seconds. Many capable men and women are disqualified from job opportunities before they open their mouths, because they simply do not *look the part.*

There are many elements of your life over which you have no control and that you cannot choose. But your external dress and appearance are totally a matter of personal preference. Through your choice of clothes, your grooming, and your overall appearance, you deliberately make a statement about the kind of person you really are. The way you look on the outside is a representation of the way you see yourself on the inside. If you have a positive, professional self-image, you will take pains to make your external appearance consistent with it.

You should dress the way the senior people in your company dress. I've told you that "Birds of a feather flock together." People like to interact with and promote people who look the way they do. Dress for the position two jobs above your own. Since people judge you largely by the way you look on the outside, be sure to look like a professional. The result will be that the perception people who can help your career have of you will be positive. They will open doors for you in ways that you cannot now imagine.

Join Professional Associations

Remember, another powerful way to increase your visibility is to join one or two professional associations connected with your business or field. Begin by attending meetings as a guest, to carefully assess whether or not a professional association can be of value to you. Determine whether the members are the kind of people you would like to know, people who are well established in their careers. Once you have decided that becoming known to the key people in this association can advance your career, take out a membership and get involved.

Most people who join any club or association do little more than attend the regular meetings. For some reason they feel that they are too busy to assist with the various jobs that need to get done. But this is not for you. Your goal is to pick a key committee and volunteer to serve on it. Find out which committee seems to be the most active and influential in the organization, and then step up to the plate. Volunteer your time, expertise, and energy, and get busy. Attend every meeting. Take careful notes. Ask for assignments, and complete them on time and in an excellent fashion.

By getting involved, you create an opportunity to *perform* for key people in your profession in a non-threatening environment. You give them a chance to see what you can do and what kind of a person you are. You expand your range of valuable contacts in one of the most effective ways possible in our country today. The people you get to know on these committees can eventually be extremely helpful to you in your work and in your career.

Donate Your Services

Join a well-known charitable organization, such as the United Way, and become active by donating your services to its annual fund-raising programs. You may not have a lot of money, but you do have *time.* Your willingness to give of yourself will soon be noticed by people who are higher up. Many men and women with limited contacts and few resources have risen to positions of great prominence by getting to know the key community leaders who participate in charitable organizations and professional associations.

Some years ago, I joined a statewide chamber of commerce and volunteered to work on its economic-education committee. As usual, very few of the members contributed any time or effort to the committee, so there was always lots of work for those few people who were willing to put in the effort. Within one year I was speaking at the annual convention for this association. The audience was composed of more than 1,000 of the most influential business executives in the entire state.

In the following year I was invited to give a key briefing to the governor and his aides at the state capitol. I became so well known in the business community that within six months I was offered a position to run a new company at triple my former salary. It all came from becoming active in the chamber of commerce and becoming known to the other members.

About three years later, I volunteered to work with the United Way and had a very similar experience. My whole business life was changed because of my involvement in helping that charitable organization in its annual fund-raising drive.

It's amazing how far and how fast you will go when you begin to give your time and energy to others on a volunteer basis. It's one of the fastest ways up the ladder of success in the United States.

Move Quickly on Opportunities

There are many other things that you can do to increase your visibility—things that don't occur to most people. For example, a study of 105 chief executive officers concluded that there were two qualities that would do more to put a person onto the fast track in his or her career than any others. The first quality was the *ability to set priorities*, to separate the relevant from the irrelevant when facing the many tasks of the day. The second quality was that *sense of urgency* I've told you about, the ability to get the job done fast.

Managers place very high value on a person who can set priorities and move quickly to get the job finished. Dependability in job completion is one of the most valued traits in the US workforce. When your employer can hand you a job and then walk away and not worry about it again, you have moved yourself onto the fast track, and your subsequent promotion and pay increase are virtually guaranteed.

Upgrade Your Skills

Recall that another way to increase your visibility is to continually upgrade your work-related skills, and to make sure that your superiors know about it. Look for additional courses you can take to improve at your job, and discuss them with your boss. Ask him or her to pay for the courses, if he or she will, but make it clear that you're going to take them anyway.

As described earlier, a young woman who worked for me was able to double her salary in less than six months by aggressively learning the computer, bookkeeping, and accounting skills she needed as our company grew. And she was worth every penny. We were happy to pay her more.

Ask your boss for book and audio-program recommendations. Then follow up by reading and listening to them and asking for further recommendations. Bosses are very impressed with people who are constantly striving to learn more to increase their value to their companies. Doing this regularly can really accelerate your career.

Develop a Positive Mental Attitude

Finally, you'll be more visible if you develop a positive mental attitude. People like to be around and to promote people they like. A consistent, persistent attitude of cheerfulness and optimism is quickly noticed by everybody. When you make an effort to cultivate an attitude of friendliness toward people, they, in return, will go to extraordinary efforts to open doors for you.

In the final analysis, taking the time to become an excellent human being will do more to raise your visibility and improve your chances for promotion than will any other single thing that you can do.

Action Exercises:

1. Commit to excellence. Excellence in your chosen occupation is the primary stepping stone to higher positions and better pay.
2. Look, act, and dress the part. Become knowledgeable about styles, colors, and fabrics. Dress the way senior people in your company dress. Never take anything for granted. Remember that in the area of image, casualness brings casualties.
3. Develop your contacts, both inside and outside the company. Network continually. Always be looking for ways to give of your time and effort, as an investment, so that others will be willing to give of their time and effort to help you sometime in the future. Begin with your professional association or club, and then join a local charity that you care about and that also has a prestigious board of directors.
4. Introduce yourself to more people. Then immediately do something for a new acquaintance. The most successful men and women in any community are those who are known by the greatest number of other successful people.
5. Take additional courses to upgrade your skills, and make sure that everyone knows about it. Ask your boss for book and audio-program recommendations. Then read and lis-

ten, and go back to your boss with your comments on what you've learned and to ask for further recommendations.

6. Ask your boss or someone else if he or she will mentor you. When your boss feels that you are eager to learn and grow, often he or she will become a mentor to you and will help you up the ladder of success. This process of being mentored, or guided, has been instrumental to the careers of many successful executives.

7. Be positive, cheerful, and helpful. Be the kind of person other people want to see get ahead. Treat other people with friendliness and patience, and always have a good word to say about the people you work with.